A DANGEROUS PLACE TO BE

A DANGEROUS PLACE TO BE

Identity, Conflict, and Trauma in Higher Education

Matthew H. Bowker
and
David P. Levine

LONDON AND NEW YORK

First published 2018
by Routledge
2 Park Square, Milton Park, Abingdon, Oxon OX14 4RN

and by Routledge
711 Third Avenue, New York, NY 10017

Routledge is an imprint of the Taylor & Francis Group, an informa business

British Library Cataloguing-in-Publication Data
A catalogue record for this book is available from the British Library

Library of Congress Cataloging-in-Publication Data
A catalog record has been requested for this book

ISBN: 978-1-78220-499-2 (pbk)

Typeset in Palatino
by V Publishing Solutions Pvt Ltd., Chennai, India
Printed and bound by CPI Group (UK) Ltd, Croydon, CR0 4YY

CONTENTS

ABOUT THE AUTHORS

Matthew H. Bowker is Clinical Assistant Professor of Humanities at Medaille College in Buffalo, NY. Educated at Columbia University and the University of Maryland, College Park, he brings psychoanalytic, literary, and intellectual-historical approaches to topics in political theory. He has published numerous papers on social theory, ethics, and pedagogy and is the author of several books on the psycho-politics of contemporary life, including: *Ideologies of Experience: Trauma, Failure, Deprivation, and the Abandonment of the Self* (Routledge); *D.W. Winnicott and Political Theory: Recentering the Subject* (with A. Buzby, Palgrave); *Rethinking the Politics of Absurdity: Albert Camus, Postmodernity, and the Survival of Innocence* (Routledge); *Escargotesque, or, What Is Experience?* (Punctum); *Albert Camus and the Political Philosophy of the Absurd: Ambivalence, Resistance, and Creativity* (Rowman & Littlefield); and *Ostranenie: On Shame and Knowing* (Punctum).

David P. Levine is Professor Emeritus in the Josef Korbel School of International Studies at the University of Denver. He holds a Ph.D. in economics from Yale University and a Certificate in Psychoanalytic Scholarship from the Colorado Center for Psychoanalytic Studies. Prior to his retirement, he held academic positions at Yale University and the

University of Denver. In addition to his work in political economy, he has published numerous books in the field of applied psychoanalysis, including most recently *Psychoanalysis, Society, and the Inner World: On Embedded Meaning in Politics and Social Conflict* (Routledge); *Psychoanalytic Studies of Creativity, Greed, and Fine Art: Making Contact with the Self* (Routledge); *Object Relations, Work, and the Self* (Routledge); *The Capacity for Civic Engagement: Public and Private Worlds of the Self* (Palgrave); and *The Capacity for Ethical Conduct: On Psychic Existence and the Way We Relate to Others* (Routledge).

INTRODUCTION

Over the past several decades, colleges and universities (hereafter referred to as "universities") in the United States and United Kingdom have made significant commitments to increasing diversity, particularly with regard to race and gender. Alongside efforts to increase diversity among students, faculty, and administration, many universities have rededicated themselves to the ideals of tolerance and inclusiveness. The result, however, has not been an amelioration of strife over matters of identity and difference. Instead, there has been continuing, if not increasing, conflict in universities, often mirroring conflict in the larger society.

In this book, we investigate a number of conflictual events on university campuses, including provocative protests and accusations directed at university members who are deemed victimizers, debates over the inclusion of "trigger warnings" on course-related materials, demands for "safe spaces," denials of venue to speakers deemed offensive, rejections of free speech as a norm governing campus interactions, and calls for the resignation or expulsion of students, faculty, and administrators. Our hypothesis is that such conflicts in universities express, with particular poignancy, difficulties encountered in the process of identity-formation. What makes the link between identity and university-based conflict difficult to see is that most controversies have been marked by efforts to ignore or disguise experiences in individuals' inner worlds and to insist on the importance of groups, group identities, and group fantasies about victimization that offer collective ("social") defenses.

In the broadest terms, recent conflicts in universities are rooted in what D. W. Winnicott refers to as the struggle between creativity and adaptation, particularly as that struggle manifests itself in the course of identity development. For the individual, this struggle begins in the family and in the home, where attachments to and interactions with significant others either foster or impede the work of shaping an identity that is rooted in self-contact and suitable for life in civil society (see Bowker & Buzby, 2017). In the world outside—and in the inner world as well—the establishment of an identity that is capable of supporting being and relating *in* and *through* difference, which includes living with those who possess distinct and diverse identities, is vital.

Identity, the family, and the group

Forming an identity involves knowing "who one is" in a way that is real to the self, and, at the same time, that can be expressed and realized in the world. Identity therefore includes "the sense of oneself as a force that matters in the world" (Bracher, 2006, p. 6). Having an identity means not only coming to know who one is, but investing value in a way of being so that being who one is "matters." Early in life, "mattering" to others—particularly to parents or caretakers—is a vital ingredient in healthy psychological development. It is necessary to know that we matter to others in order to secure the feeling that we matter to ourselves. Affirming for infants and children that they matter requires appropriate forms of attention, attunement, and love. We will refer to these activities as "appropriate forms of care." Appropriate forms of care attend to the child and not to caregivers' emotional needs, anxieties, or defenses. Appropriate forms of care affirm expressions and behaviors that are creative and spontaneous, rather than those that are adaptive and ritualized. Appropriate forms of care respond to expressions and behaviors that originate in the child rather than outside.

Taken together, appropriate forms of care affirm the child's sense that he matters in himself, and that he may dare to be himself and to realize himself in fledgling attempts to define and enact his identity, first within his family, and later outside. For this process to be effective, it is not necessary that the child's expressions or activities receive solely positive responses from caregivers, only that the presence of the child's self, which is to say his distinct being and the internal source of his activity, be confirmed in interactions within the family. As Winnicott might say, even if there is to be a clash or a battle between child and adult, if there is a "richness" in the interaction then family members may find in the experience an opportunity for emotional growth and identity development (1971, p. 145).

Appropriate forms of care support the development of a positive investment in the self, which allows a positive investment to develop in the concrete form the self takes in the world: its identity. The failure to provide appropriate forms of care, on the other hand, is experienced as a rejection of the self and makes a positive investment in the self and in its concrete form difficult or impossible. This situation leads to the formation of an identity that is disconnected from the self, or, at least, is problematic in terms of its connection to the self. The identity adopted in the context of failures of care is one that rejects the self as the source of being, doing, and relating. This identity is linked to what Winnicott terms the "false self."

The family home is the first place where the individual truly matters. Ideally, the individual matters to the family not because of her utility in the family organization, or because she plays a role in the family particularly well, or because she affirms the experiences, beliefs, or fantasies held by the family. Rather, she comes to matter in and for herself. Within the concept of "appropriate care," therefore, lies the concept of appropriate protection *from* the family. The family that permits its child to matter and, in so doing, facilitates the development of a healthy and authentic identity, protects the child from impingement and coercion. That is, the family provides a form of safety for the child, one that secures the child's sense *that she is* and *that she can be*. R. D. Laing termed this "ontological security" (1969, p. 33): a sense of reality in one's thoughts and feelings and a belief in the safety of bringing forth into the world what is real in the self.

Of course, in many families, children are not afforded "ontological security," for their survival is made contingent on exhibiting particular attributes, fulfilling specific tasks, or behaving according to a set of expectations set by caregivers. All (or virtually all) children live with rules, tasks, and obligations. But some are not only confronted or disciplined when they violate the expectation that they adapt to family demands, they are threatened with a loss of connection to the family on which they depend.

We might ask why families and caregivers would put their children into such precarious positions, positions in which it is *dangerous to be themselves*. The answer would be that caregivers and families often, perhaps typically, suffer from a belief in the essential badness of the self. For them, contact with the self provokes feelings not of safety or vitality, but of guilt and shame. Such families seek to protect their children from guilt and shame by preventing them from being themselves and from developing identities that might expose their bad, shameful selves, not to mention the bad, shameful selves of other family members. While it is beyond the scope of this chapter to explore the many sources of guilt and shame within individuals and families, shame, in particular, is commonly instilled by the same inappropriate forms of care intended to protect against it. That is, shame and inadequate care for the self are mutually constitutive.

The (frequently unconscious) effort to block contact with the self employs both shame and self-destroying forms of guilt associated with aggression against caregivers. While guilt is not inherently destructive, when it develops into a dominant aspect of self-relating and forms an essential element in the child's sense of who he is, rather than serving the process of self-development and the formation of an identity expressive of the presence of the self, it prevents contact with the self.

Families and caregivers operating under the assumption that the child's self is "bad" will offer what might be called "inappropriate forms of protection," inasmuch as these protections do not protect the child from demands for adaptation, but, rather, "protect" the child from herself. In lieu of being herself, the child is offered or ascribed a false self, one typically associated with family "pride," which operates as a defense against unconscious identification with the bad self. This inappropriate form of protection, then, condemns the child not only to shame but to profound confusion about her real self, about who she really is and who she might be. Since neither the child nor the family are consciously aware of what is happening to self and identity in this situation, negative feelings associated with the bad self are projected outward, onto individuals, groups, and organizations outside the family. These others are imagined to be responsible for the child's (and the family's) shame, or are made to be carriers of it.

As the child matures, he may come to expect or demand *in*appropriate forms of care and *in*appropriate forms of protection from the groups and organizations of which he is a part, particularly if those organizations present themselves as facsimiles of his family home. He will expect these organizations to concur with the fantasies and defenses erected early in life and relied on throughout maturation, since these fantasies and defenses have helped to prevent him from knowing what he suspects to be true about his self: that it is bad, shameful, and unworthy of love. He will expect the groups and organizations he joins, in other words, to protect him from himself. The more, then, that a university takes on the look, feel, and functions of a family home where inappropriate forms of care were the rule, the more it blurs the line between past and present, between reality, memory, and fantasy, and between life in the family and life outside. The more a university presents itself as a family home for students, the more it encourages students to demand from it a form of care associated not with the feeling of security in being, but with "protection" from the desire to express the self authentically. In other words, the university will protect its members from the presence of their selves. And the more those in the university identify with students' false selves and engage in comparable defenses against contact with their own original vitality, the more the university will collude with the work of the family to suppress or hide the child's—now the student's—true self, no matter how much emphasis is placed on the student's "safety."

Where the situation just described governs psychic life and determines the nature and aims of relating, experience outside the family will take on the meanings associated with early family experience. In particular, settings outside the family (such as school and work) will be treated as opportunities to re-enact an internalized drama of family life in which the self was treated as a bad object and subjected to exclusion and attack. The more powerful this internal drama, the more likely that all experiences, even those that do not follow its script closely, will be interpreted on its terms. In re-enactments of internal dramas, early experiences of inappropriate care are represented (re-presented) in the adult world, in adult language, and as present-time experiences of victimization and oppression.

For the adult, or young adult, there can be *both* real, present-time experiences of victimization and oppression, *and* experiences interpreted in this way because of the power of internal dramas to guide, shape, or fit experiences into familiar schemas. In the university, both possibilities are in play and it is difficult, if not impossible, to determine the balance of the two in any given circumstance. Because of this, students' accounts of having been victimized, oppressed, or traumatized should neither be dismissed simply as aspects of fantasy life, nor accepted simply as reality-based accounts of contemporary experience. They may fall into either category, or, more likely, they may represent a mixture of the two.

One of the most important settings in which relating is organized with the purpose of hiding the self and replacing a self-determined identity with one disconnected from the self is the group, especially the group organized to establish a group identity for its members. The driving element in group identity is the re-enactment of the family relationship through which a parent or caregiver defined the child according to an identity that was not the child's own. In this book, we speak about this process as the imposition or ascription of an identity, an identity shaped without regard to the child's true self, her original vitality, or her "unique presence of being" (Bollas, 1989). The group engages the individual's (self-destructive) impulse to adapt to the family's imposition of identity. In doing so, the group and the individual work together or collude to serve the group's primary aim, which is to secure and deepen members' attachment to the group and to assure the adoption of its shared identity.

To the extent that the family is also a group, the imposition of identity on the child there is the signature example of the imposition of group identity. Indeed, the family is the first and ultimately most important group to which the individual belongs. Furthermore, the family is a social institution of its own, charged with raising children in ways consistent with the family's interpretation of social expectations. The family is, then, both a group unto itself and a socializing group, tasked with helping the child develop an identity in accordance with several sets of (often competing) demands.

When the child internalizes the conviction that his self is essentially "bad," he requires a false or adaptive self to protect him from the resulting experience of shame. The false or adaptive self prevents contact with the bad self and, at the same time, prevents the bad self from exposure in relations with others. Participation in group life can play a vital role in supporting false self systems and in protecting individuals from awareness of their bad selves. When the group serves this end for its members, it creates what has been referred to as a "social defense," which is a defense that uses a social system, organization, or institution to manage experiences that might cause emotional suffering (Menzies, 1960). When social defenses take the form of socially defined identities and socially defined interpretations of relating—in other words, the outlooks or schemas that shape the meanings of interactions with others—the emotional suffering associated with an internal assault on the self can be externalized. That is, negative feelings of shame about the bad self can be projected onto others outside the group.

The counterpart to this imposition of shame on others is the celebration of the group identity as a source of pride. Here, defending against shame means taking pride in an identity that is, by design, severed from connection with the self and from the individual's own agency and initiative. In other words, the social defense, or group defense, against shame actually validates the worthlessness of the self and affirms the importance of adopting an adaptive or false self organized around an ascribed group identity. Taking pride in group identity protects the group member from identification with a bad self but, at the same time, reinforces that very identification. The resulting tensions and ambivalences play vital roles in the kinds of conflicts in universities with which we are concerned here.

The individuals and groups involved with the issues treated in this book struggle with a significant measure of anxiety. On the surface, their anxiety appears to be about others' perceptions of their identities. At a deeper level, however, their anxiety is rooted in the fear that repressed knowledge of themselves will be brought into awareness. In an attempt to allay this fear, they seek to control others' perceptions of them, a strategy sponsored by the projection of the repressed self onto others. In other words, the anxiety at issue here is anxiety about what will be known about the self by self and other. If the university was once a place (or was imagined to have been a place) where a fortunate person could come to "know himself," it is not clear that today's universities, students, or faculty still value this function. Thus, the place of the university and the nature of its work must also be considered if we are to understand the meaning of conflicts rooted in identity and in how the self and others may be known.

The place of the university

For centuries, the university has played a unique role both in the lives of students and as a "transitional" institution between the family home and the civil society. As something of a gateway between the worlds of family and civil society, part of university life has traditionally involved students' discoveries of and struggles with the friction between these worlds, particularly between the distinct expectations and responsibilities to be found in each. Because of this, universities are suitable settings in which to examine conflicts between the norms governing life in the family and in civil society.

By calling the university a "transitional institution," we mean not only that students have typically attended universities as part of their journeys from home life to engagement and employment in society, but that the nature of the university has, at least until fairly recently, been conceived as an organization that temporarily "holds" and protects its members from at least some of the demands of the world in which they will later live and work. This separation of the university from the outside world once conferred on the university a kind of "privilege and authority within the social order" that served as a foundation for what Robert Nisbet refers to as the university's bestowal of a "sense ... [of] liberty" on its members (1971, p. 16).

Today, however, we are witnessing a degradation of this separation of the university from external institutions and a corollary weakening of the university's boundaries. We may even say that the university is at the height of an "identity crisis" of its own as it struggles to adapt to the pressures of a competitive higher education "market," the needs of non-traditionally aged and first-generation students, and, perhaps most importantly, demands arising from students, community members, governments, funding agencies, and other constituencies that it become a different kind of organization than it has been in the past. We are primarily concerned with one subset of these demands: the demands set forth by students and protestors that the university undertake significant organizational change because, according to them, the university is a dangerous place.

By forcing the resignation of staff touched by scandal, by shying away from conflict with students or groups who claim to have been victimized in the university, and by failing to defend the boundaries of the university itself, university leaders have colluded with the assumptions underlying protestors' demands and have, ironically, only enlivened conflict and strife on their campuses. What seems to motivate the university to undertake collusive responses when faced with identity-based conflicts is, ironically, a fear of losing control of how it will be known by others and, therefore, of how it will know itself. This dilemma, which is a primary theme of this book, is one in which a struggle to maintain control over (both individual and organizational) identity contrasts with the reality that the power to determine "who one is" has already been ceded to others.

As we have already suggested above, central to understanding conflict in universities is their relationship to the complex, emotionally invested, and ambivalent notions of "home" and "family." The importance of this relationship is evinced in the frequency with which these terms are used to describe university life as, for instance, a "home away from home" (see e.g., Delgado-Guerrero, Cherniack & Gloria, 2014; Reagan, 2013; Strayhorn, Terrell, Redmond, & Walton, 2010), or a "family of learners" (see e.g., Kafele, 2013; Southall & Bohan, 2014). Part of the complexity of the relationship between university and home derives from the place occupied by schools in general, and universities in particular, in the individual's transition from the family to society.

Developmental psychologists have sought to recognize this in-between state of university-aged individuals in the West by suggesting an intermediate stage of life between adolescence and adulthood. "Emerging adulthood" (Arnett, 2000), as it has come to be known, now defines the stage of life (from eighteen to twenty-five years of age) during which individuals complete those "developmental tasks" once associated with adolescence. Foremost among these is contending with the often competing needs for "autonomy" and "connectedness" (see Diamond, 1991; Harter, 1999).

More than sixty percent of "emerging adults" in the United States now enroll in institutions of higher education, a greater percentage than ever before (Arnett, 2000, p. 471). What is more, defenders of the uniqueness of this developmental period argue that, due to a host of demographic and socio-economic changes in post-industrial societies, it is no longer adolescence but emerging adulthood that is the period of life in which individuals find "the most opportunity for identity explorations in the areas of love, work, and worldviews" (p. 473). Even "non-traditional-aged" students—those over the age of twenty-five—share some identity attributes with emerging adults, since they invest money, time, and labor in redeveloping their personal, professional, and civic identities.

But data suggest that students are now entering university with identities whose processes of formation have more or less come to a halt (Hettich, 2010, pp. 93–94; Shaffer & Zalewski, 2011). Whereas the university was once imagined to be a place for exploration, experimentation, identity "moratorium," and self-discovery (see Marcia, 1967; Tobacyk, 1981), it seems to have become a place where individuals with fixed or firmly established identities seek to confirm what they already know to be true about themselves, others, and the world. In this quest for conformation, some elect to do battle with those whose senses of self and other differ from their own.

At the same time, the social, cultural, economic, and political functions of the university have undergone substantial changes in the past half-century. In contrast to the vision of the university as an "Ivory Tower," a space set apart from and above the concerns of life outside, the university today has become a socially integrated organization, one that considers itself dependent on, and obliged to, the communities, markets, and populations it serves. Community partners, service organizations, or even employment agencies might be better descriptors for contemporary universities than esoteric towers of ivory, aloof from the cares of the world. This change in orientation, however we may judge it, has brought with it a fair amount of disorientation and role-confusion for students, faculty, and administrators.

We believe that the term "Ivory Tower" is a poignant metaphor for what lies at the center of conflict in universities today. The notion of an "Ivory Tower" suggests a firm boundary, even a kind of fortress or citadel, in which those who are unable to defend themselves can nevertheless feel safe and secure. The metaphor, then, alludes to the protection children are meant to be afforded from a world made dangerous by the fact that they are not yet physically or emotionally prepared to cope. But the height, color, and purity of the image of the 'Ivory Tower' also suggest a reaching upward, toward light, or toward enlightenment. The link between security and reaching upward may tell us something important.

One possibility, consistent with the line of argument in this book, is that what we "reach for" when we reach "upward" is something akin to the self, variously expressed in such notions as enlightenment, wisdom, and freedom of thought and expression. Reaching upward, then, also means reaching inward, toward an inner spirit or self. Consistent with this idea are connotations of the term "Ivory Tower" that suggest a secluded place in which practical matters can be treated in an impractical way. So, just as the term suggests the defense of a boundary, it also suggests "liberty" from another kind of boundary: the boundary that separates what can be imagined from what can be done in the world outside imagination. This boundary is coincidental with the boundary between the inner world and the reality principle, which is experienced by some (particularly by children) as tyrannical, since it is the boundary that limits the boundlessness of the imagination.

These considerations map onto the relationships between childhood, adulthood, and society, and, therefore, between play, reality, and work (Levine, 2010; Winnicott, 1971). What play, especially the play of imagination, is to childhood, work is to adult life. It is useful, then, to consider struggles in universities as struggles over the boundary between imagination and reality, between the inner world and the world outside, between play and work, and between the child and the adult in a state of transition from childhood to adulthood.

These struggles play themselves out in the university as struggles over the ability of the university to know and defend its own boundary, which is the boundary between what goes on inside—teaching and learning—and what goes on outside—work and civic life. The boundaries of the institution need to be understood in relation to self-boundaries, indeed as the external form those self-boundaries take. What is at stake in struggles within the university is nothing less than the security, even the possibility, of *an inner world*, the defense of which is the defense of the life of the mind, and the defense of the capacity for imaginative construction. It is, therefore, the defense of the possibility that the individual can carry forward into adult life something essential about childhood experience: the capacity for creative living, or, in somewhat more oblique language, the capacity "to create the world" (Winnicott, 1986).

It needs to be emphasized that this is no simple struggle between those working within the university and those outside. Rather, it is a struggle that has been internalized. This internalization of struggle within universities parallels the internalization of the struggle within the individual, which shifts from a struggle over the reality principle between child and parent (or child and teacher) to a struggle within the individual. The individual's internalization of this struggle means that important figures outside now have a presence inside the mental life of the child and, later, the student, taking the form of figures acting out roles in an inner drama. This inner drama then becomes the basis for enactments in the world outside. If it is the individual's inner world that has become a dangerous place to be, then he must "turn himself inside out, to dramatise the inner world outside," in order to "save himself" from dangerous forces within (Winnicott, 1990, p. 89). Such dramatizations or enactments take the form of the conflicts with which we are concerned here.

While learning institutions come in varying shapes and sizes, and while the pace of change among them differs, the typical university has held on to an organizational culture in which relationships with its primary constituents—relationships between students, faculty, administrators, and staff—are distinct from those of other social and political institutions, such as the family, the corporation, the government agency, and other organizations in civil society. One of the most obvious ways in which this uniqueness has manifested itself is in the vicissitudes of the doctrine of *in loco parentis* (a legal construct from the Latin, meaning: *in the place of the parent*) as it has been applied, contested, and, in some cases, reinstated in American universities. Some offer persuasive arguments that recent protests calling for university officials and leaders to "regulate … students' personal lives—including speech, association, and movement—and take disciplinary action against students without concern for the students' right to due process" (Lee, 2011, p. 66) undermine earlier generations' struggles to emancipate themselves from such forms of social control by university representatives (Soave, 2015).

Further on, we consider in more detail the meaning of university interventions in the private lives of students. For now, we observe that university students are considered to be relatively autonomous adults: They are held responsible for their own coursework, for their grades, for their conduct, for ensuring that their tuition payments are received, and the like. At the same time, however, students are treated as children or adolescents. Students are "taken care of" by universities to a great degree, and today's students find themselves catered to by an ever-growing assortment of services and amenities that either imply or state outright that students need and want greater university intervention not only in their educational pursuits but in their personal, professional, and social lives.

The increasingly popular ideal of "student-centeredness" in higher education has an ambivalent meaning in that it expresses a regard for the student as an individual, but, at the same time, is used to justify a form of catering to students—which is really catering not to the student but to the adolescent in the student—that some find infantilizing:

various forms of academic support and "academic coaching" services, elaborate recreational facilities, 24-hour support hotlines, "graduation guarantees," and myriad opportunities for "engagement" and "involvement" that embed the student in campus and community life.

Such trends, particularly initiatives that offer "personalized" attention and the enhancement of students' sense of "engagement" with the university, reflect the desire of university leaders to forge identifications between students and the university, identifications that tend to bolster student enrollment, retention, and, later, alumni participation. Today, a top priority for student-service staff is convincing students that most, if not all, of their needs, desires, and goals, even those having little to do with formal education, can be met in connection with the university. Put another way, the priority is in making a place that feels, at first, like a "large," strange, new environment "feel like home" (see Boyington, 2014).

Even as students' expectations of university support are stoked by promises of flexible, student-centered, entertaining, and accommodating university experiences, popular and academic discourses about the poor preparation of today's students hold that students lack what it takes to survive in the "adult world." Recent "diagnoses" of millennial and post-millennial youth as lacking "grit" have become increasingly fashionable (see Duckworth, Peterson, Matthews, & Kelly, 2007). Peter Gray argues that "young people ... [are] going to college still unable or unwilling to take responsibility for themselves, still feeling that if a problem arises they need an adult to solve it." Citing a past president of the Association for University and College Counseling Center Directors, Gray agrees that students today "don't seem to have as much grit as previous generations" (2015).

Attributions of weakness to students are sometimes employed to justify efforts to apply "tough love," to break students out of their intellectual "comfort zones," and to expose them to the "hard and fast" realities of adult life, which is the life they are imagined or expected to face after university. Accusations of students as childish and weak work to establish a narrative about education that suggests that exposure to "the real world" (Barack, Mintz, & Emba, 2014; Svetlik, 2007) is needed if graduates are to thrive in the society that exists "beyond the campus walls" (Courtney, 2009; Moore, 2015). But such efforts make the experience of university life confusing for students, who at one moment are offered countless forms of support and personalized attention, some aimed purely at facilitating their entertainment, and the next moment are accused of belonging to "Generation Me," a uniquely and dangerously "narcissistic" lot, unprepared to survive the harshness of an adult life in which no one will attend to or care about their needs (Twenge, 2006; Twenge & Campbell, 2009).

It has become all but routine for educators in the United States and elsewhere to be entreated—in campus addresses, teaching workshops, or institutional initiatives—to liberate students from their "narcissistic" self-orientations, which are thought to be correlated with low levels of "intrinsic motivation" to study (Deci & Ryan, 1985), by connecting learning experiences inside the classroom to experiences outside the classroom, in "the real world." These "real world" experiences are imagined to motivate and prepare students for the type of social labor that awaits them upon graduation (see Curtis, 2001; Kolb & Kolb, 2009). Today, some students spend significant time engaged in community-service projects, many with unclear pedagogical relevance, while other students find that the "real world" has overtaken their classrooms, which are no longer assemblages of desks and chairs but are "interactive learning spaces" and "collaboratoria," outfitted with "interactive technologies" and designed to maximize interaction and technology-assisted group participation.

Michael Godsey relates a few truly memorable examples of how "classroom environments that embrace ... social learning activities are being promoted now more than ever," to the detriment of students, some of whom are "easily drained by constant interactions with others." For instance, the University of Chicago library announced recently that "in response to 'increased demand,' librarians are working with architects to transform a presumably quiet reading room into a 'vibrant laboratory of interactive learning'" (2015). Similarly, Dartmouth's Institute for Writing and Rhetoric has challenged its students to "forego passivity in favor of contribution and participation," apparently because, unbeknownst to many writers, writing is "a communal act," not a "private isolated one." Indeed, the website explains, "students must overcome isolation in order to learn to write" (Dartmouth College, 2015).

These discourses and practices, even with all of their contradictions, may be understood if we regard the focus on shaping students' experience of the university not as an effort to liberate students from their "narcissistic" orientations, but as an attempt to realize an ideal of the university as an organization that serves society, whether "society" be taken to mean the business community, the public sector, or the world of non-profit organizations dedicated to moral-political purposes associated with social justice. If a university successfully "corrects" the putatively ego-centric orientations of students by enticing them to replace self-seeking with activities that promote enmeshment with the needs of educators, institutions, and communities, then the university believes it has accomplished its mission.

To put it in a stark light: A problematic trend in recent efforts to change the "place" of the university may be understood as the university's attempt to sever the student's connection with the self, in part because, as we have already discussed, anxiety and shame associated with beliefs about the badness of the self have been projected onto—and, in many cases, internalized by—students. As will be discussed in more detail in Chapter Four, this aim is also motivated by an experience of narcissistic injury suffered by university faculty, staff, and administrators in the increasingly deprived and depriving environment of higher education, where the work conducted in universities is afforded less and less intrinsic (or non-instrumental) value. The dilemma faced by the contemporary university is passed on, as it were, to students, such that students are now permitted, persuaded, and sometimes coerced to take on pursuits whose aims are not their own. It is this attack on the student's self that links together the seemingly opposed views of students as vulnerable individuals in need of support and protection and, contradictorily, as egotists in need of "grit" to be produced by subjecting them to the harsh realities and "hard knocks" that will prepare them for what is imagined to be a cruel and unforgiving world outside.

Understanding and neutrality

The debates with which we are concerned in this book involve highly charged clashes of opinion, especially opinion shaped by implicit and explicit moral judgment. Public discussion of struggles in universities has featured, on one side, strong condemnations of students for being unable to deal with adversity and aggression in however mild, or seemingly mild, a form. On the other side, morally tinged epithets have been directed against universities and university members for being "racist," "sexist," "misogynistic," or in other ways discriminatory, for enjoying "privilege," and for putting students in harm's way. Noticeably absent has been a serious effort to understand, rather than to judge, these events and the individuals and groups involved with them. Put another way, what has been missing is a pursuit of understanding as something *other* than a basis for moral judgment.

In our interpretation of recent struggles in universities, we rely on the idea that understanding offers something different than (and more than) a grounding for moral judgment. In developing this idea, we recognize that the pursuit of understanding, detached from moral judgment, means giving up certain benefits and protections garnered by offering or affirming moral judgments. It also means taking on the risk we will become targets of those who insist on making moral judgments at the expense of understanding. It is also possible that our comments will draw the ire of those who contend that understanding is inherently oppressive, that, in the words of Albert Camus, "he who has understood reality… becomes a conformist" (1956, p. 156; on understanding as betrayal, see Bowker, 2014).

By emphasizing understanding, we reject Camus' assertion and, instead, call upon Freud's comment on analytic neutrality: "It is certainly possible to forfeit … success if one takes up any other standpoint than one of sympathetic understanding, such as a moralizing one, or if one behaves as the representative of advocate of some contending party" (quoted in Laplanche & Pontalis, 1973, p. 271). Rather than align ourselves with or oppose "some contending party" in university conflicts, we strive to give voice to what Winnicott refers to as the "true self," which is the individual's original vitality or presence of being. If, in treating these matters, we are to apply understanding in the hope of giving voice to the true self, we cannot impose beliefs, ideals, or aims on individuals, but must respect the need for a space within which the individual can make the expression of being in doing an end in itself (Levine, 2013).

The sort of judgment that is particularly adverse to the work of understanding is not judgment on the merits of various political positions or even on matters of university policy, but judgment, whether hidden or overt, on the merits or virtues of the participants in struggles over those issues. Problems arise in making this distinction, of course, because the difference between judgment of the merits of policy and judgment of the moral standing of individuals and groups tends to be obscured by the way that judgments of policy are experienced as judgements of a person's or group's moral standing. This confusion is also linked to the effort to make virtue and moral standing the ends of policy, whether this effort is carried out explicitly or implicitly.

Groups seek moral judgment as a way of assuring alignment between judgments made by those inside the group and judgments made by those outside. This alignment reinforces a sought-after internal judgment on the part of group members by making what would otherwise be a subjective self-assessment an objective fact. This wished-for transition from subjective to objective is the essential element in the relationship between internal and external judgment and plays a central role in university conflict. Thus, a group of students might insist that the university accept its charge that the university is a racist institution because acceptance of that charge would make the group's subjective experience—the experience of living in a world of others who have harmful intent—an objective fact. Now, internal, negative self-assessments can become external events and relationships involving the denigration of group members by those outside the group.

We might be tempted to treat the university's acceptance of culpability, in this example, as a simple matter of providing support for members of oppressed groups against long-standing denigration of their identities. That is, we might be tempted to consider what we will later refer to as "compassionate" behavior a simple matter of helping individuals and groups fend off the imposition of negative judgments of their worth, expressed, for example, in degrading racial or ethnic stereotypes. Certainly, in some instances, this is the case. But, in addition to historical or present-time experiences of denigration in relations with others, we must also acknowledge the presence of problematic internal self-assessments, where the sought-after taking of responsibility by those outside the group replaces a negative self-assessment with one that defends against the feeling that the self is of little value.

When those in the university but outside the group accept responsibility for the negative feelings of group members, the negative feelings are replaced with others having a more positive valence. Denigration of group identity is transformed, if you will, into a celebration of the virtues of group members, virtues understood, in some instances, to be derived from the experience of denigration itself. But, a difficulty arises here that is of special importance for understanding the consequences of various responses to university conflict. When those outside the group align themselves with the favorable self-assessment overtly sought by individuals in the group, they are likely also aligning themselves with unfavorable internal judgments held at the unconscious level. That is, favorable external judgments are sought as part of a defense against profound doubt about the virtues of group identity. The intensity of the need for favorable judgments of identity by others may therefore be considered a measure of the intensity of the doubt about group identity within the group. And, as a result, the bad feelings associated with the denigration of group identity may be exacerbated by the very relationships established to defend against those bad feelings.

The issue just raised is closely related to the matter of "analytic neutrality," briefly alluded to above. "Neutrality," in this sense, does not refer to any prohibition against analysts having political convictions and, in the arena of public life, acting on those convictions, but rather against the analyst making statements that might be experienced in the analytic setting as aligning the analyst with the patient's internal objects and the self-judgments associated with identification with those objects. When we speak of replacing judgment with understanding, we have in mind something analogous to analytic neutrality, since we seek to avoid basing our assessment of university conflict on judgments of the moral worth of individuals or groups. Specifically, we do not, by endorsing either a favorable or an unfavorable moral judgment of any group or individual, engage in an act that, however unconsciously, colludes with a defense against powerful unconscious feelings that the self embedded in the group is of little value.

Approaches that collude with internal objects and judgments support defenses against identification with denigrated internal objects. In so doing, they protect the power of those objects in their work against the self. They reinforce the danger to the self that began as a harshly critical self-judgment. There is a way of approaching the problem of judgment that does not involve collusion with internal objects and judgments in this way. We suggest that university conflict be engaged in terms of the consequences of different policies for the safety of the self *in the inner world*; in other words, in terms of whether the policy pursued strengthens identification with bad internal objects and the harsh self-judgment associated with it, or, rather, strengthens the self by weakening identification with bad objects and the power of the negative self-assessment provoked by it.

Concern with the safety of the self in the inner world is expressed in the proposition that the analyst should not impose his values on the patient nor offer "unquestioning acceptance of the patient's values," that the analyst not "try to bring about a certain kind of change because he believes in it in principle," and that the "analyst [be] non-judgmental not only with respect to the patient, but also with respect to others in the patient's life" (Greenberg, 1986, adapted from Schafer, 1983). Translated into the context with which we are concerned here, the implication is that universities should neither impose morally invested ends on students nor offer unquestioning acceptance of the moral judgments students espouse, and that universities, instead, should facilitate internal development in a direction consonant with understanding and self-determination.

The stance suggested here implies a kind of neutrality in university conflict: neutrality with regard to the moral standing of parties to that conflict. This neutrality is needed because of the way the idea of morality inevitably involves the division of those engaged in conflict into the "good" and the "bad." This division is precisely the goal of the harsh self-assessment to which we have referred, which, by its nature, allows little if any room for nuanced understanding of human motivation beyond that which is organized around good and bad choices driven by good and bad character. Indeed, this "moral orientation" is the expression of the work of harsh internal object relations experienced as a harsh internal self-assessment.

The ideal of support for the self stands opposed to the ideal of the university as a moral training ground, devoted to preparing students for their subsequent entry into life in a moral order (on moral order, see Levine, 2017). It should be noted that, so far as the goal of education is taken to be strengthening the student's harsh internal self-assessment and the flight from the self it implies, the kind of neutrality we recommend may well be considered the *enemy* of the educational enterprise. We argue that the attack on neutrality in the university constitutes a form of collusion with unconscious self-denigration, which, in turn, stands in the way of achieving any educational ends linked to strengthening the student's capacity to make "doing express being," to paraphrase Winnicott.

With these considerations in mind, we can identify two distinct and opposed ideals for education. The first involves the work of assuring that students are prepared to lead a life consonant with the idea of a moral order, the life of a member embedded in a moral order who subordinates her self to the group. The second involves the work of facilitating the development of the capacity for a life outside a moral order, in a civil society. University struggles can, then, be understood as struggles over whether the purpose of education is to embed the individual in a moral order. And, so far as embeddedness in a moral order is the end of education, university struggles may be understood as struggles over which groups within that moral order will be identified with the good.

The struggle over who will be identified with the good develops and intensifies in settings where groups that bear moral standing are defined along lines of race, ethnicity, gender, or religion. In the ideal of civil society, individuals exist independently of their group identifications. In conflicts in contemporary universities, then, we see elements of a broader struggle between two visions of life: life in a moral order and life in civil society. Thus, in the world of the university, the question is not only which individuals or groups will be identified with the good, but whether the good will be assigned to particular groups at all, and whether pursuit of the good held by groups will be the overriding end of the life students are expected to lead when they graduate.

Outline of the work

We have introduced our project as one that treats a small and illustrative, but in no way exhaustive, sample of controversial events concerning issues of identity in the university. Our goal is not to judge students', protestors', or university members' activities in themselves, but, rather, to understand what these activities signify. We apply psychoanalytic insights to these events with the hope of understanding them as enactments of a dilemma involving the process of identity formation and the discovery of difference in the self and in others.

In the first chapter, we reflect on a case of a controversial art project undertaken by a student at the State University of New York, in which "White Only" and "Black Only" signs were placed around campus near formerly shared spaces, such as bathrooms, elevators, water fountains, and benches. This example is helpful in considering the two fundamental ways of knowing the self and others considered throughout the book. One way of knowing affords us the ability to discover what is different about ourselves, while facilitating our capacity for resilience in the face of demands for adaptation to others' needs. The other way leads us to regard the world as a dangerous place, where those who differ from us intend to do us harm. The temptation for university officials and leaders (as well as some faculty and students) to be drawn into re-enactments of the kind created by this student, rather than to understand and communicate about them, spells trouble for the kinds of enlightened dialogue and civil engagement one might hope to find on university campuses and, later, in civic life. In this chapter, we also discuss the important difference between empathy and compassion, and its relation to identifications that bind students to groups, and that bind groups to faculty and administrators. These identifications tend to reinforce the problems underlying protest and conflict, while blocking measures that could better serve the needs of students.

In Chapter Two, we explore the debate over what have become known as "trigger warnings": notifications offered to students in anticipation of encountering explicit or provocative material in a university setting. Whatever the incidence of trauma, in the narrow sense of the term, on university campuses today, we find a tendency toward *vicarious engagement* with trauma and identification with victimized groups. One may assume the identity of a traumatized victim, of course, if one has been a traumatized victim, but one may also assume that identity if traumatized victimization is a central part of one's identity or of the identity of a group to which one belongs. In either case—and the two are not mutually exclusive—as a result of their association with earlier loss of safety in being, what may seem, to some observers, to be minor events on campuses are, to others, deeply distressing experiences.

Even if conflicts on university campuses are frequently entangled with internal dramas involving emotional abandonment and denigration of the self, we cannot dismiss responses to perceived hostility as evidence of "hypersensitivity" or "overreaction." There may well be real hostility between groups who define themselves as victims and others as victimizers; indeed, part of the goal of enacting dramas of victimization is to make them real in the world. We are not interested in delegitimizing accusations or complaints about (re-)traumatizing events in the lives of students or other university members. Rather, we wish to understand why such a great variety of experiences involving suffering and distress have come to be identified with traumas and why individuals and groups seem increasingly interested in incorporating the concept and language of trauma into their identities and activities.

In Chapter Three, we consider restrictions on speech and expression in the form of demands for "safe spaces" and in student movements such as "No Platform," which advocates denying venue to speakers deemed offensive by some part of the university's constituency. The need to silence others, even—or especially—before they have spoken, stems from a need to control their power over the vulnerable self, as well as a desire to recoup losses associated with an earlier silencing of the self. Such experiences and their subsequent re-enactments turn individuals to groups and organizations whose fantasies reinforce, rather than resolve, core psychological conflicts.

In this chapter, we focus on the distinction between two kinds of freedom of expression. The first is the freedom to use speech to impose a denigrated identity. This makes freedom of speech a license to assault. The second is the freedom not just to speak, but to think our thoughts. The second kind of freedom emphasizes freedom from harshly imposed internal prohibitions on our thoughts. This is freedom of speech and thought as an internal matter: the freedom to speak freely about our-selves to ourselves.

In Chapter Four, we examine the role of the university, as an organiza-tion, in facilitating, resisting, or exacerbating the kinds of conflicts with which we are concerned. We first consider the university's increasing enmeshment with the wider community, an enmeshment that erases boundaries between the university and the world outside and suggests a radical redefinition of the place and function of the university in relation to both students and society. We then reflect on attempts by the univer-sity, undertaken for a variety of reasons, to act as a surrogate family home for students. By assuming home-like qualities, we argue, the university colludes with students' efforts to re-play or re-enact roles and dynamics present in their families and their internal worlds. When the two types of boundary erosion are combined, the university risks becoming an organization that exploits students for its own benefit, while providing inappropriate forms of protection that deny students opportunities to engage in the university's primary work of teaching and learning.

We conclude by arguing that the ideal of diversity is driven by a complex and ambivalent fantasy. This fantasy entails contradictory meanings of the concept of diversity as, on one hand, a norm govern-ing spaces that embrace difference and, on the other hand, a demand that groups and communities bound together by identification and sameness be given place within the university. Of course, the dilemmas associated with diversity, when understood in this way, are not limited to matters of race, ethnicity, or gender, nor are they limited to the uni-versity. Rather, they express fundamental ambivalences, rooted in the maturational process and in challenges involving early encounters with difference, about the possibility of creating a meaningful and valuable identity in the university and, later, in civil society.

CHAPTER ONE

Private space, resilience, and empathy

The prominence of moral judgment in campus controversy is closely linked to *how* participants come to know the moral standing of those with whom they have entered into conflict. Indeed, there is a sense in which moral conflict is all about our way of knowing self and other. Let us consider a basic distinction between two ways of knowing. In one, knowing is the result of a process of engagement with an object that is not already known, and which, therefore, may be different from those we already know. In the other, objects have all been previously encountered, and our task is to determine with which, among the already known objects, we are currently dealing. Those who know in the second way hold a set of preconceptions they use to know objects, so that the problem of knowing becomes a problem of determining which preconception to apply. Knowing others in this way means insisting on the reality of preconceived qualities of objects, often by using aggression to assure others' acquiescence to our preconceptions. In other words, when we have recourse to the second way of knowing, knowing others means assuring that others be what we need them to be.

As a prime example, we will reflect on the (graduate) art student at the State University of New York who posted "White Only" and

1

"Black Only" signs by elevators, drinking fountains, benches, and bathrooms across her campus in an effort to make unseen racism visible. In the words of the art student, the project was intended to serve as "a reminder that just because you can't see racism around you doesn't mean it's not there" (Foran, 2015). Of course, such provocative signs calling for racial segregation were likely to remind Americans of the history of Jim Crow laws and other forms of discrimination.

Due to confusion about who posted the signs and what message they conveyed, there was a swift "backlash" against the incident and a subsequent "tense debate over racism and free speech" at the university that continued for several months after the signs were taken down (Foran, 2015). The student who created the signs remarked that this reaction among university members—a reaction involving fear and anger, among other powerful emotions—was precisely her point. "I wanted people to feel something," she said. "I wanted people to realize they must confront racism and fight against it in their daily lives."

For our purposes, what is most remarkable in this account is the student's insistence, which is by no means unique to her, that racism exists even in the absence of visible manifestations of it. That is, if racism involves negative judgments or harmful intentions directed at others based on their race, then a student who claims that racism is pervasive and invisible is making a broad claim about the inner worlds of others in her community, about the victims of racism (who are, in this case, persons of color) and about the (presumably white) perpetrators of racism.

In response to this claim, we could challenge the student to present more definitive evidence of racism or to otherwise defend her position. Doing so, however, would involve us in a drama in which our denial of the presence of racism might be taken as evidence of its presence. This possibility is discussed in further detail below. For now, we offer the related observation that by engaging the student in this way we would likely be returned to what has already been communicated, which is that this student's knowledge about racism comes less from an investigation of the external world, and more from an inner conviction. After all, this student's contention that "just because you can't see racism around you doesn't mean it's not there" is expressed in the form of a preconception. Indeed, the most tangible evidence of racism at the university at that time, the "White Only" and "Black Only" signs, were posted by her. It might even be said that this student created the evidence of the racism she insisted was present.

To be sure, this student encourages us to see her judgment of her fellow students and her university's culture as one grounded in experience and not in preconception. In explaining her actions, she indicated that she was forced to deal with racism earlier in her academic career, while attending another university, where she "was called a 'n—monkey.'" She also spoke of "generational" struggles that she, along with "many non-white people currently living in America" experienced in her family (Chan, 2015). We know little about this student's particular family experience or about her experience at the other university in question. Even if we did, we would still have to ask how this student moved from her personal experience to a broader assessment of the beliefs and attitudes held by members of a (large) organization and even about entire classes of people. Since this student has cited earlier experiences of overt racism and struggles related to racism in her family as evidence of the (hidden) presence of racism in her new university setting, we may speculate that her movement from personal experience to broader judgment regarding the attitudes of others is really a movement from internal to external, one in which she uses her personal experiences as a template for determining what she knows about others, even about those with whom she has no personal connection.

The communication this student offers to fellow university members is a complex one. Clearly, it involves the effort to tell others how she feels: surrounded by unseen racism. It involves telling them that her relations with those whose skin color differs from hers are shaped by a conviction that what they observe when they see her is the color of her skin, and not the person she is. These others know her, we might say, without getting to know her, but this knowledge of her is really a knowledge of a degraded self linked to her race. Of course, her communication is also an attempt to tell us that this personal experience is not, in fact, personal, but shared, objective, and real. And this assertion seems to ground her desire to make others "feel something," which we might understand as the desire to provoke in others feelings similar to those she has experienced and to draw others into the "confront[ation]" and "fight" with which she, herself, is engaged.

Private space

One way to speak of the link this student draws between internal and external is to focus attention on her art project as an enactment. What we have in mind by using the term "enactment" is that she is engaged in establishing relations with others in the university that create the external reality of an internal drama, and that others are placed into roles and are encouraged or provoked to behave in ways consistent with the script of her drama. Enactment, understood in this way, is a method of communication, much like the method used by a playwright putting on a play. Through the vehicle of the play, the playwright communicates something to the audience. Similarly, through her enactment, the art student communicates something to her fellow students and teachers, except that, in the case of her enactment, the audience and the players are meant to be the same.

We can respond to the communication embedded in the enactment in two ways. The first is by playing the roles scripted for us, the roles into which we are enticed. Or, we can attempt to understand the communication and, as part of doing so, resist the pressure to become players in the student's drama. Responding in the first way, we might accept our role by knowing ourselves, as the student knows us, either as hidden racists, if we are white, or as victims of hidden racism, if we are "non-white." Alternatively, we might reject the roles ascribed to us in this drama, regardless of our skin color. But, as alluded to above, insisting, for instance, that we are not racist can also mean participating in the drama so far as doing so may be taken to affirm that we are "hiding" our racism and are thus oblivious or indifferent to the pain felt by victims of hidden racism and, in that way, that we are contributing to it. What might appear, then, as resistance to taking on a role may actually indicate acting *in role*, which, in the case of a white person who rejects the attribution of "racist," means indifference to the plights of black students and disavowal of responsibility for their plights.

The alternative to acting in role is neither to embrace nor reject the role of the hidden racist, but to attempt to understand the communication about racism offered in the form of a drama. What might this understanding look like? What is overt and explicit in the enactment is the insistence that there are people in the world (represented here by white members of the university) who wish, for example, to have separate bathrooms for themselves, bathrooms to which black students are not admitted. But this is not all. In the enactment, black students also have separate bathrooms, bathrooms of their own to which white students are not admitted. In the student's enactment, then, there may also be a wish for a separate bathroom, although this wish is not expressed directly.

Following this line of thought, we can consider the theme of the enactment to be that of exposing or exhibiting a hidden desire, the desire for a place of one's own. This desire must be hidden, even from the student herself, presumably because there is something unacceptable, even dangerous, about it. If this is the case, then the communication of the drama via its enactment is about both a desire and a need to hide that desire. In the drama, the hiding of desire takes the form of transferring it onto white university members, who are thereby made vulnerable to the danger associated with the prospect that *their* hidden desires to have places of their own will become known. Thus, the author of the enactment does not experience the desire for a separate place of her own as her own desire, but as theirs, and in this way keeps it hidden in the very act through which she reveals it.

In this drama, the wish for a separate bathroom likely plays a special role because of its link to intimacy and privacy. To the extent that this link is operative in the enactment, the student's communication would appear to be an attempt to convey a loss of personal and private space. This would not be an unreasonable assumption for a university student, even a graduate student, who finds herself living in a shared space, subject to the kind of forced intimacy university life often entails. University living, for many students, means a loss of private space and entry into a world shared with strangers.

While this loss of private space may be all too real for students, to understand the enactment with which we are concerned here, we also must consider what is held in private and what is in danger of exposure if there is no private space to hold it. If what is held in private is the hidden self, then this enactment involves the wish to exhibit the hidden self, the shame felt in doing so, and the need to hide this wish and this shame by locating them outside, in others (on the hidden self, see Levine, 2017; Winnicott, 1965). Put another way, at the center of the drama is the wish to feel pride in a hidden self for which, instead, we feel shame. This shame results from anxieties concerning the exposure of our hidden selves to strangers, represented by those whose skin color differs from ours.

In the art student's drama, the complex struggle over matters of hiding and exposing, pride and shame, takes the form of a struggle over aspects of bodily experience: race as expressed in a physical fact and the need for privacy as expressed in the need to have a private space. While we might take these matters literally, it is likely that both race and intimacy have a more complex meaning in which the physical dimension is only one aspect, used to represent a reality irreducible to it. Indeed, the prominence of matters of pride and shame points us away from the physical dimension and in the direction of aspects of being that have to do with the value we invest in personal or private being. The term often used to refer to personal being, especially the personal being at stake in the struggle over pride and shame, is, of course, the "self." We could say, then, that an important problem with which the student seems to struggle is the reduction of her self to a physical fact about her.

The reduction of self to physical being is central to struggles in universities. This reduction makes all that is of value in our personal existence a kind of brute fact about us, something given to us at birth that can never be changed: the self as skin color. In a language used by Christopher Bollas, this reduced self is the self dominated by its "fate," rather than the self as the active moment in pursuit of its "destiny" (1989). In a sense, the struggles in universities over identity are struggles over whether students must submit to their "fate" or can, instead, pursue a "destiny" not predetermined by ascribed or imposed qualities of being, qualities as immutable as those that define their physical existence.

This construction of the problem allows us to develop a distinction already implied in our discussion of the hidden self. This is the distinction between two selves, one hidden and one to which access is made available. The self that has been equated with, or reduced to, race is a self made available to others, indeed, a self created *by and for* others. This is the self we have when we submit to our fate. The more we are identified with this self, the more we must keep hidden any qualities of being inconsistent with it, qualities that develop when we insist that who we are is not determined by factors such as culture or biology. Submission to fate brings with it the hiding of the self, which is tantamount to psychic death.

Struggles over the standing of the self expressed in the language of race can also be seen on a more general level in debates about "institutional racism," a notion that has been invoked especially in connection with concerns about black students' access to spaces, cultures, and communities of their own, distinct from what is described as the overarching "white" culture of the university. Clearly, this concern is closely linked to the wish for a private space from which others are barred. In his discussion of institutional racism, Claude Steele observes (quoted in Green, 2016) that schools offer black students the opportunity to assimilate into an alien, or white, culture. But, to do so, they must "give up many particulars of being black—styles of speech and appearance," and thereby "learn how little valued they are." Following this line of thought, Adrienne Green notes the "uncomfortable campus climates" for black students and discusses the toll these climates take on their mental health. Her emphasis is on the added burden felt by black students due to what Ebony McGee describes as the way they need to weather "the cumulative effects of living in a society characterized by white dominance and privilege [that] produces a kind of physical and mental wear and tear that contributes to a host of psychological and physical ailments" (quoted in Green, 2016).

An account of the problem consistent with the line of thought developed above draws attention to the idea that black students feel they do not belong; and they feel they do not belong because the world of the university is not their world. If this is the case, it is understandable that they would respond by wishing that it could be made their world; for example, by offering them more faculty who "look like" them (Lovell, 2014), a demand that has been voiced by numerous students and student groups. The importance of having teachers who "look like" us stems from a construction of the world in which what people look like is the most reliable clue as to how they think and relate—that is, whether they think and relate like us. If those who look like us also think and relate like us, then being with them places us in a familiar world.

In the absence of people who look, think, and relate like us, being in the world means giving up the familiar world we inhabited before university; it means the loss of home. And living in an alien world has consequences for our ability to place a positive value on our own world. As Steel insists: "For too many black students school is simply the place where, more concertedly, persistently, and authoritatively than anywhere else in society, they learn how little valued they are."

In this assertion, whether we are valued or not is made a matter of our race and of the value placed on the culture argued to be associated with it. We may wonder, however, if the problem is not so much, or not only, about the value of culture, but about the attachment of the individual's self-worth to the worth of her culture, which is then understood as a matter of the value attached to her race. This attachment leads to a notion of "institutional racism" that has the following meaning: the failure of an institution (in this case the university) to offer those in it a replication of the safety of a world they inhabited before coming to that institution, which is the safety of a world populated by people who are like us. But, was this world really "safe," and would the replication of it really advance the aims of higher education? We will not get very far in exploring this matter if we assume from the outset that the answer is yes; instead, we must treat it as an open question.

We have suggested that the term "institutional racism" refers to the fact that the university does not provide black students with a space that feels like "home," which is a private space in which the hidden self might emerge. In part, the concern expressed here may be a more general concern with the way the world outside the home—that is, "civil society," is not a place in which the hidden self is welcome or safe. In Winnicott's way of speaking, civil society is not a place in which it is safe to *be*. If this is an important part of the message, then concern about racism is one expression of a more general concern about the opposition between private and public—intimate relations and relating to strangers. It is a concern expressed in the habit of treating personal experience as the template for relating to those with whom we have no personal connection.

But, it is also possible that "home" refers more to a fantasy or myth of safety and intimacy than a reality, and not only for students of color. When home was *not* a safe place to be, then the pursuit of safety in a world where everyone is like us becomes problematic, because it was the people who were most like us who made our world (the family) an unsafe place to be. This is the intolerably dangerous thought we must not think. Thus, it is not only the thought that home is not a safe place that must be blocked, but the desire correlated with that thought, which is the wish to make contact with our hidden selves.

If the people who are "like us" have made our world an unsafe place for us to be, they have done so by demanding that we be "like them." This demand implies that what is unsafe in the world is the desire to be ourselves, to be in contact with our hidden selves, to be different and to be present. We will understand this dimension of the problem better if we consider more closely the matter of how we know self and other and whether our process of learning who we are is essentially a process of adaptation to others' expectations that we be "like them."

Resilience and adaptation

One possible implication of the loss of private space is that this loss is essentially about the loss of identity, where identity is equated with being embedded in a group culture. In the case we have been considering, this group culture is defined by race. But, there is another possibility, which is that the protest against hidden racism, while couched in the language of race, racial identity, and race-based culture, is about something more general, which is the demand for adaptation itself and the resulting loss of self-determination implied in adaptation, *no matter what group culture demands the adaptation*. If we are to consider this possibility, we need to look more closely at the consequences of adaptation. Here, we consider adaptation as a relation between the internal and external worlds, one in which what is inside the mind adapts to what is outside in a way that threatens private space in a fundamental way.

In exploring the idea of exposing hidden racism, we have emphasized the way those who experience hidden racism gain knowledge of the minds of others. In attempting to understand the kind of knowledge involved, as well as the way of knowing self and other implied by it, we have suggested that the way we know others is shaped by the way we know ourselves. What this means, more concretely, is that if we insist that the attitudes of others are determined by *their* race, then this offers evidence of the attitude we hold regarding ourselves, which is that what we know about ourselves is what we know about *our* race. So, those who experience unseen racism know the minds of (white) people independently of what those people say and do (i.e., independently of their experience of them) because that is how they know their own minds; because, for them, that is how all minds are known. But this method for arriving at self-knowledge does not develop by accident, nor is it inevitable. It is an internalization of a way of being known that was the defining element in early childhood experiences of self and other. If the most important people in our lives when we were growing up knew us independently of their experience of us, then that is how we came to know ourselves, and that is how we know others.

Being "already known" to significant figures in our growing-up experience places us in the position of having to adapt to what is already known about us, to become what others already know we are. Early in life, we have no resources to resist this external determination of who we are. Because becoming an adult, in this situation, means adapting to a pre-existing role or model, there is little room for engaging in a process of self-determination that would help us define what is uniquely our own. And if becoming a person means adapting to a role or model, then doing so is not about establishing ourselves as a distinct or unique person existing in our own right. Rather, the moment of adaptation is the moment in which we discover that everyone is the same; in other words, that we need make no connection with the unique circumstances and trajectories of others' lives in order to know them.

Of course, there are ways we wish to be known and ways we fear to be known. We may wish to be known as strong, competent, admirable, and morally good. We may fear we will be known by the absence of these qualities. To the degree that our self-knowledge is determined by how others know us, the way others know us controls our own sense of who we are and of our qualities of character. Thus, we require an ability to control the way others know us, so we can know ourselves in the ways in which we desire to be known. The more this situation obtains, the more the ability to control others becomes the essential element in our relationships with them.

What gives moral judgment its emotional force is the ability of the parties that would judge us to make us know ourselves in the way they know us, to make us racists by saying that we are, or to make us experience our race as a mark of inferiority because they see it that way. If struggles on university campuses are power struggles, this is the real power at stake in them. The power of others to determine what we are by saying what we are is only real if it gets inside our heads, so to speak, and exerts control over what we know about ourselves. If others hold this power, they hold it because we have been taught from an early age to see ourselves through the eyes of others, to adapt ourselves to their expectations, and to cede this power to them. If there is shame and humiliation involved in this relationship, it stems ultimately from the loss of self-determination implied by others' ability to take control of our minds. That is, shame and humiliation exist, in this situation, because others have assured us that the (only) way we may know ourselves is by finding out what they know about us.

It is not, however, inevitable that self-knowledge be derivative of the way we are known by others. We may also develop *resilience* in the face of the pressure put on us by assessments coming from outside. We are resilient when we stand up to or resist external determinations of who we are. We can be resilient if we can turn away from others who would define us and find inside a capacity to know who we are independently of their efforts to know us.

In other words, resilience develops alongside a secure identity and sense of self, which is, in turn, the product of a growing-up experience in which we did not have to adapt to survive. The less we feel we must adapt, the more we feel free to discover and define who we are, and the more we exist in the world as a separate and distinct center of initiative and action. To enable us to achieve this end, our parents need do nothing but resist the temptation to know us ahead of time and check the related impulse to seek their own feelings of security in discovering the ways in which we are the same as they. As Winnicott puts it: "The parents do not have to make their baby as the artist has to make his picture or the potter his pot, the baby grows in his or her own way if the environment is good enough" (1965, p. 96).

This development of resilience in the self is not complete but ongoing for students in universities. And, for many students, trends in the opposite direction, toward adaption, are already too advanced and too powerful for resilience to develop. If the individual's family experience has been one of adaptation in the sense described above, there is little a university can do to reverse the course set in motion there. In any case, it is not surprising that students in universities struggle with the interplay between seeking to know themselves through assessments offered by teachers and by fellow students on one side, and, on the other, securing and exercising the resilience that would provide a degree of real security about who they are, apart from how others see them.

Resilience is about the existence of the self as an enduring structure, about the experience of a continuity of being in and through activities, experiences, and relationships (Kohut, 1977). When there is a continuity of being, there can also be a presence of the self and manifestations of this presence knowable to others, which is what we speak of in the language of identity. But identities may also be constructed *not* to express our unique presence of being but to meet the expectations of others, to display a self that is designed by others and made admirable by the fact that others admire it.

When who we are is shaped by external expectations, it is possible to know others without having had an experience of getting to know them. This is because who we are reflects only external expectations shared by our reference group, a group that assures us that we lack the kind of uniqueness or distinctness that would make knowing us require an effort to get to know us. But, while we gain recognition and even admiration in this way, we also feel diminished when it is possible to know us without getting to know us. We are diminished because there is nothing important to know that uniquely pertains to us, which means that, in a fundamental psychological sense, we do not really exist, at least not as a person in our own right. Rather than existing in our own right, we belong to those in whom we invest the power to know, define, and judge us. When faced with this situation, control over the way others know us becomes a vital element in our interactions with them.

In thinking about conflicts over race in universities, we have placed special emphasis on the way our identity is given to us, imposed, or ascribed. Focusing on matters of ascribed identity suggests another way of thinking about the art student's engagement with her fellow students, teachers, and university members. Her act of putting signs on bathrooms, water fountains, elevators, and benches could be understood as a way of taking on an identity defined for her by teachers, fellow students, and the larger community. This is an identity defined by the act of revealing or "calling out" unseen racism and speaking up against a racist culture. This identity is, in some ways, complex, in that it derives both from personal experience and from the impulse to connect to a group.

Earlier, we noted the link between personal experience and assumptions about qualities of broader groups or classes of people. Here, personal experience in a limited setting becomes something universal: Some white students at one university become all white people at all universities, and perhaps elsewhere. Personal experience, and the way we generalize from it, empowers us to know what is in the minds of others. In other words, it is not the experience taken in some irreducible sense that matters, but the way the experience is generalized and interpreted.

But experience takes on meaning not only in the context of the individual's personal life, but also in a context of interpretations provided by a group and by figures in the larger culture with whom the individual identifies. Because there are two sources of meaning, there can be inner conflict if the two meanings contrast sharply. This is especially the case when the personal meaning involves shame, while the meaning later attached by identification with a group dismisses this shame and attempts to find in an experience originally interpreted (however unconsciously) as shameful a source of pride. Then, the process of identity formation seeks to replace a humiliated child with a strong young person. The experience of suffering and victimization is reshaped into an identity organized around the ideal of strength and empowerment.

Central to the identity formed in this way is the feeling of existing in a dangerous world. After all, the attraction of the identity, for example, of a "strong black man" or a "strong black woman" lies in the way strength and aggression are needed to cope with life in a dangerous world. For those drawn to identities such as these, danger is associated with the presence of people unlike us in the world, which means that danger arises from difference. Were there no difference, there would be no feeling of danger. That is, this identity relies on the conviction that what makes us different (e.g., our race) both puts us in danger *and* gives us strength.

This way of understanding what makes us feel endangered can help us understand something about the celebration of difference that is such a large part of university culture. The effort to construct what makes us different as a source of strength can be traced to the important part played by convictions about a dangerous world, which is a world in which survival depends on strength, especially the strength to meet aggression with aggression and to turn the tables on those imagined to put us in danger. But if we follow this line of thought, the more we empower difference, the more dangerous the world becomes. Because of this, empowerment of difference is both a solution to and an important part of the problem.

To return to our example, we hypothesize that the result of the art student's personal experience and of the meaning she has invested in it is that, rather than developing an identity that expresses her unique presence of self, she occupies an already defined role that assures her a place in a group. By taking on this role, she gains security at the cost of self-presence. If this is the case, then her art project is a ritualized enactment of a predetermined identity. In itself, this does not make her message about invisible racism true or false, but it does make it complex in that we can understand it not only, or even primarily, on the level of the overt claim it makes, but also on the level of the identity it allows her to occupy. The more powerful this latter purpose in driving the enactment, the less it matters whether her overt claim about racism is true or false, and therefore the less important it is that we respond to the message on the level of the overt claim.

If we are to judge enactments of this kind as assertions of identity rather than as political interventions, then what is important in them is not the empirical validity of propositions such as "Racism is everywhere," or "The university is racist," but the connection of the identity enacted by it to self-determination. We can, of course, make this connection a moral issue. And, indeed, doing so is inevitable when the identity enacted is about securing group membership by occupying a well-defined role (e.g., an empowered, courageous, strong black woman). In other words, by enacting a designated role, individuals place themselves on a moral plane and make identity a moral issue, just as they make the identity of those different from them a moral issue, in this case by defining their identities in an enactment exposing hidden racism.

By insisting that white people are racists independently of what they do or say, the art student claims that they are morally bad because they are white. This severs the link between their moral standing and their agency (or self-determination) and insists that all white people must be, in some sense, as she is: occupants of roles disconnected from their wills, rather than centers of initiative in their own right. Like the art student, the white people implicated in her project are victims of an imposed identity carrying a substantial moral burden. Indeed, all of the issues with which we have been concerned can be understood to depend on the way in which an imposed identity also imposes a kind of moral burden.

Morality can play a large role in separating what we do and how we relate from agency and self-determination. This happens when morality constitutes a shared belief system designed to regulate living. The more powerful morality in regulating how we think and what we do, the more doing and relating become enactments of predetermined rituals. Thus, for instance, the more religion exists for the member of a religious community as a set of "right" ways to behave and "right" thoughts to have, the more identity is given to us by our group, and the less we exist for self and others as a unique presence. This link between moral standing and group ritual can have much to do with the emphasis placed on the alienation of some students from university culture and the necessity that alternative cultures be made available within the university.

Alternatively, the regulation of conduct can be made to follow an ideal of respect for the unique presence of being we associate with self-determination. Then, the ideal is that of our presence in what we do and how we relate to others, rather than our adaptation to roles and enactments of the rituals that define those roles. Ambivalence about identity develops when there is an internalized conflict between the impulse to be present and to make our identity express self-determination, on one hand, and the demands for adaptation associated with group membership on the other. From the standpoint of the demands of group membership, expressions of self-determination constitute attacks on the group, which inevitably judges them to be morally bad. Because it is the involvement of the self in shaping identity that moves it away from enactments of group-sanctioned rituals, the group's moral judgments of self-determined identity and expression are essentially moral judgments of the self. Ambivalence about identity, then, develops as an expression of ambivalence about whether the self or the group should be the active factor in defining who we are, what we do, and how we relate to others.

Intent to do harm

Although it may seem counterintuitive, one of the most important forms of control we attempt to exert over others is knowing that they hate us and wish to do us harm. We can see how this might be the case if we consider what would happen if those who experience a world of unseen racism were to allow for the possibility that others whom they do not know (in the example of the art student: white university members) do not hate them. In asking this question, it is not our intention to claim that the idea of hidden racism is incorrect, but to consider the nature of the insistence that evidence and experience need not be taken into account when assessing the validity of beliefs about others, and to consider how this insistence, whether correct or not, may express the need to know that one is hated by strangers.

The conviction that (white) people hate others based on their race is well-protected from counter-evidence by the insistence that their hate exists even if it is invisible. We have argued that this conviction and its protection suggest that knowledge of the minds of other people may reflect an internal or psychic reality that expresses a powerful emotional need. The art student's enactment would seem to confirm the hypothesis that one way of knowing and relating to others—a way organized around attributions of hidden hatred—is driven by the need for them to hate.

To explore this hypothesis further, let us highlight an aspect of the way of relating embedded in this enactment that has not yet been made explicit. This is the aspect of causation. If we take, as our starting point, students' feelings of living in a dangerous world, and if we accept that these feelings are real, we still need not assume the same is true about the way students interpret their feelings as the natural result of the presence of others who intend them harm. While some may feel endangered because people in their world *do* intend to do them harm, there are other possibilities as well. For instance, they might feel this way because of any number of impersonal threats, such as the possibility of failure in school or in their future career, the possibility of failure and loss in personal life, and so on.

An important feature we can see in much of the conflict in university settings is the way those involved interpret their situations on the basis of a fundamental conviction, which is one we will refer to as the power of subjective causation (Levine, 2017). This is the conviction that subjective intent rules the world; that, to find the cause of our inner emotional experiences, we must look to others who intend for us to feel the way we do and who have the power to make us feel that way. What we find most notable about the decision to attach anxiety, for example, to the presence of white people in the world is the way it identifies an external agent, or a set of agents, as the source of danger. In other words, thinking in this way attributes the source of anxiety to the intent of a particular group of people, or, more precisely, to the intent of individual members of that group. If we have a reason not to take this choice at face value, it is the same reason already considered: It demands that we know what is in the minds of people we do not know. This, in itself, offers prima facie evidence that we do not simply find ourselves in a world where people in fact intend to do us harm, although they may, but rather that we have a need to attribute our anxiety to the intent of strangers, rather than to consider alternative sources.

When we follow the path toward self-knowledge that relies on being known by others, we are particularly vulnerable to the presumption that our anxiety has its source in the way others see us, because, along this path, we have already accepted the premise that others hold the power to enter into our minds and to determine what goes on there. It is unsurprising, then, when those who relate to others in this way attribute their anxiety to the presence of strangers with harmful intent who are imagined to be capable of inflicting significant harm simply by holding disparaging thoughts or beliefs about them. To deal with this situation, it is necessary to try to control the world outside in a way that limits the presence of those strangers, and, where this is not possible, to attempt to control what those strangers say and think.

The heightened anxiety central to the mental processes described here is not limited to the individual but is shared among many, if not all, students. As we have intimated above, there is much about higher education that provokes anxiety for students: being away from home, negotiating more adult relationships, including sexual relationships, contending with pressures to succeed in what is at least perceived to be an academically challenging environment, preparing for a professional life in the world outside the family, and so on. All of these possible sources of anxiety have one thing in common: They do not emanate from the presence in the world of individuals or groups with the intent to do harm. They are better understood as internal challenges organized around hope, fear, and self-doubt. They are closely linked to the fact that students are still in the process of establishing the resilience to which we refer above, and are therefore still vulnerable.

Collusion, compassion, and empathy

Most students in universities are at a crucial moment in their emotional development; a great deal depends on how the organizations in which they find themselves engage that moment. Organizations may either support students' efforts to develop the resilience they need to free themselves, to some degree, from their dependence on others to define them, or they may deal with students' vulnerabilities in ways that block the development of their autonomy. Which direction the organization takes depends on whether it colludes with students in the interpretation of their anxiety about personal development as anxiety about the harmful intent of others.

We will discuss collusion in the university in more detail in Chapter Four, but, for now, it is important to note that faculty and administration collude with students when they agree that they are the source(s) of students' anxiety, most notably because they are different (in this case: white), and therefore intend harm (in this case: are racist). In doing so, they affirm the explanatory system of subjective causation employed by students. This explanatory system impedes the development of students' capacities to experience and understand sources of anxiety that do not involve persons with the intent to do harm. It impedes their development of notions of causation that are not subjective and, perhaps more importantly, precludes reflection on the possibility that it is not others but rather dynamics embedded in their inner worlds that are responsible for how they feel about themselves.

Colluding with students in this way also serves the emotional needs of those designated to occupy the role of victimizers in students' enactments. Central to understanding the conflicts with which we are concerned is the need on the part of faculty and administrators to take on the role of what, in psychoanalytic language, would be referred to as a "bad object." One way to understand this form of collusion is to see it as an effort to protect the innocence of the students, freeing them of culpability for destructive acts undertaken as part of their effort to protect themselves from the dangers they perceive. This dynamic applies particularly to students from groups that have been victims of discrimination and exclusion. What sets the dynamic in motion in these cases is the attachment of victimization to innocence.

By taking on the role of the bad object, faculty and administrators affirm the innocence of victims. But, for this to work, the students must be assigned the role of victims, and the question remains: Why assign them that role? An obvious answer is that they are assigned the role of victims because they *are* victims. Proceeding in this way would mean, for example, assigning black students to the victim role because they are black and because all black people are victims, regardless of the particular circumstances of their lives. In other words, it would mean consigning all black people to the role of objects determined by others, rather than subjects determined by themselves. Doing so would be consistent with the method used by those students who know white people to be victimizers and who insist on the obduracy of racial difference, which means that what people think and do is determined by race and not by anything distinctive about them.

If we follow this line of thought, it leads us to the conclusion that just as black students in our example need to find people in their world who hate them for being black, white people in universities need to find people in their world who are victims because of their race. More precisely, white people in universities who see themselves as racists need people in their world who are designated as victims by their group identities. We need victims for the same reason we need people to hate us: because we feel that it is too dangerous to acknowledge our own victimization, just as it is too dangerous to acknowledge that our hate originates inside; in other words, that we are hateful. Thus, as painful as it may be to see ourselves as victimizers, it is better than seeing our own victimization, just as it is better to have someone hate us than to acknowledge that we are hateful. Then, just as the black students are using white students, faculty, and administrators as containers for the threatening power of hate they experience in their world, so also white students, faculty, and administrators are using black students to contain their own victimized selves.

Psychologically, we are all drawn to being the victimizer rather than the victim and, at the same time, we are all drawn to the role of victims. We are drawn to the role of victimizer first because of the empowerment implied in being the victimizer, and second because of the possibility of undertaking reparative acts that can undo that harm, reparative acts that also indicate empowerment. Reparation does not dismiss the unconscious wish to harm the innocent, but it offsets the moral damage to the self stemming from that wish. That is, it allows us to keep hope alive that we may become worthy of love. On the other side, we are drawn to the role of victim because of an inner conviction about our innocence and the injustice of our role as victimizer, even when we have, ourselves, embraced that role.

The power of the impulse to do harm, to be the victimizer, makes the individual susceptible to accusations of being responsible for the damaged self of victims. Indeed, it may make those accusations welcome, at least unconsciously. In this case, the two parties to the relationship collude: White university members (particularly faculty and administration) welcome accusations of responsibility for harm done for which putatively victimized students seek an external source in the subjective intent of others. If we feel shame for our own victimization, and lose the positive investment in the self that is the purpose and result of that victimization, then we need to expel our victimized selves onto others, whom we would also protect from the danger we pose to them. In addition, we feel guilt because, unconsciously, we wish to do harm. So, taking on the role of the racist white adult, for example, fits an internal drama. Accepting that all white people are racists accomplishes something similar to what the art student in our example has done: universalize a personal experience as a way of alleviating the intense shame that would be felt if the experience were treated as uniquely her own. There is, then, a complex identification established in this drama between victims and victimizers and between students of color and (white) university leaders.

Put in another language, we may say that collusion with regard to the interpretation of students' anxiety constitutes a *compassionate* connection with them. Compassion, typically valued and even valorized in university settings, refers to an emotional connection organized around identification. While we may experience compassion as an expression of care for others, the reality is made more complex by the role projection plays in shaping identification. When projection plays a significant role, those for whom we feel compassion act as external containers for qualities of ourselves we can only relate to at a distance. Although these are vital aspects of ourselves, because there is a danger felt in acknowledging them, we feel safer finding them outside. Once we have found them outside, we can enter into a relationship with those designated to contain them, which is really a complex form of a self-relation.

This complex relationship develops, for example, when we cannot safely acknowledge our vulnerable, impaired, or abused self, but can attempt to nurture that self as it exists, or is imagined to exist, in others. An important form of compassionate connection in university life involves we call the "fantasy of the oppressed." Universities that collude with students engaged in identity-based conflict (such as the art student's provocative enactment) find in identification with a fantasy of the oppressed a way to manage unacceptable aspects of the self-experience of white university members. But because such identification and collusion involves the acting out of a reparative fantasy, and not an engagement with the reality of students' situations, it places students who protest (in this case: black students) in a double bind. On one side, it gives into demands stemming from students' insistence that others take responsibility for their anxiety. On the other side, because it gives into students' demands, it denies the reality of their circumstances and the complexity of their inner worlds.

The need to establish compassionate connections follows from the danger felt in acknowledging our own impaired and abused selves. The danger associated with this stems from the passivity implied by impairment, which is, ultimately, impairment in the ability to act as persons in our own right, to be independent, to take initiative, and to be responsible for who we are and what we do. If these capacities are impaired in some way, and if we are forced to acknowledge that they are, then the result is a feeling of shame. The powerful discomfort associated with shame can foster a search for impairment in others, which can take the form of what we refer to as identification with a fantasy of the oppressed. The more we can find impairment in others, the less acutely we feel it in ourselves.

When we are engaged in an identification of this kind, our attribution of our own oppressed selves to others enlists them in our fantasy life. This creates a gap between the reality of others and our experience of them, which is as containers for our impaired selves. The presence of this gap makes the connection with others *not* a connection with what is real and true about them, but with who they are as occupants of a role in our fantasy. Operating in this way, a white person might very well respond to the art student by accepting her judgment that he is a racist. Doing so would establish a relationship with her based on collusion with her effort to communicate, or transfer, responsibility for her feelings of persecution. But, this compassionate response would also affirm the student's need to rid herself of bad feelings about herself, especially shame, by making others feel shame. It would affirm her conviction that whatever disparaging feelings she has about herself are caused by the hateful thoughts and actions of others. By affirming the urgency of the need to rid herself of bad feelings, it would affirm the power of those feelings, and, in this way, the compassionate response would have an effect diametrically opposed to what we typically imagine to result from it.

The stronger the identification with an individual or group, the greater the pressure to accept—without question—the interpretation of its condition, an interpretation that holds the group together. To be more precise, it is not just the interpretation but the moral judgment embedded in that interpretation that solidifies the group and its predominant fantasy. Because compassion shares a fantasy of oppression, rather than liberating individuals from the damaging consequences of oppression, it ties individuals all the more tightly to those consequences by interpreting them as their opposites.

Unlike compassion, *empathy* refers to a connection with an individual or group that facilitates movement away from the group's fantasy of itself and toward understanding of the group member's real situation. The empathic (or empathetic) connection accomplishes this by forming a connection with disavowed aspects of self-experience, rather than with the fantasy put in place to avoid contact with what is felt to be an unacceptable self. Empathy, understood in this way, refers to "the understanding of what is rejected, what is feared and hated in the human being" (Racker, 1968, p. 32).

Empathy offers understanding in place of judgment and, in this way, does not serve the interest of the group, insofar as the group is interested in allocating good and bad, guilt and innocence, shame and pride. Indeed, the purpose of the group is to prevent empathic understanding of self and other: of self because of the fear that understanding the self will mean knowing that it is not good but bad, and of other because we are best assured we will not know our own degraded selves if we can transfer them outside, onto others.

The distinction between empathy and judgment directs our attention to an important aspect of struggle in universities, which is the surprisingly intense *resistance to empathy* evident there. After all, if the judgment of others is used to cope with aspects of our self-experience, it will be dangerous to enter into relationships in which that experience may be acknowledged or made known. If empathy involves a relationship in which we are known by others, then the emphasis on judgment can be considered a strategy to defend against empathy.

Let us consider an example that will likely be familiar to those who work in university settings. During a classroom discussion of the Holocaust Museum in Washington D.C., a student made the following statement concerning the possibility of understanding the experience of others: "If you are not black, you cannot understand how I feel." Up to that point, the conversation had been mainly about how the Museum was designed to communicate to visitors something of the experience of being transported to a concentration camp and, therefore, about how it attempted to convey, in a limited sense, an understanding of an experience to those who had not had that experience.

In response to this interpretation of the Museum's mission, the student insisted that no such communication or understanding was possible, suggesting that the white students and teacher "cannot understand how it feels to be black." The aggression attached to her statement brought the conversation in class to a halt, and, in part because of this, the teacher was drawn to the conclusion that the student's statement that others cannot understand how she feels was meant to convey a somewhat different message: "You *must not* understand how I feel." By effectively stopping the conversation, she validated her own assertion, since she prevented the class from any attempt to understand how she feels.

We can imagine different reasons this student might work so hard to prevent an empathic connection with her experience. It may be that she assumed such a connection would reveal to others self-feelings, such as shame, that she could not tolerate acknowledging. Alternatively, it may have been that in seeking to block understanding she sought to protect her group identity as a black person, on the premise that allowing others to understand what those in her group feel and experience would threaten the group's existence, which depends on reserving for members access to its unique, defining emotional elements. The two explanations may not be mutually exclusive, especially if feelings such as shame are important in defining the group's experience.

This student's intervention was an example of the use of aggression to prevent an empathic connection, experienced as threatening. That connection would be threatening if it involved, even in a limited way, the reproduction of an agonizing experience of shame. Her unstated message, then, may be that to have shame acknowledged by others is to be shamed by them. In other words, empathy is feared to generate the (disavowed) experience it seeks to understand. The equation of empathy with producing undesirable or untenable experiences makes empathy a dangerous form of connection.

But this equation only holds if empathy involves a higher-order processing of experience such that the experience can be understood. Those who experience intolerable self-states such as shame are often ready and willing to share them, so long as doing so does *not* lead to understanding, since understanding requires that the experience be accurately located in the source of the projection rather than in its target. Understanding, then, returns the projection to its original source, although not necessarily in the form it had when projected outside. Processing the communication and then returning it to its source means that empathy is not, in fact, a threat of the kind imagined by those seeking to protect themselves against it. That it is not such a threat, or at least need not be, does not however mean that it is not imagined or experienced to be a threat.

This student's experience of the prospect of being understood suggests two things about empathy. First, empathy is a relationship of a particular kind and, therefore, can be welcomed or rejected depending on the psychic meaning the individual gives to relatedness with others. Second, empathy as a form of relatedness has a setting appropriate to it, and it may be rejected because the setting is felt to be inappropriate (Pao, 1983). These considerations will be taken up again in the following two chapters, concerning trigger warnings and vicarious trauma, and safe spaces and free speech, respectively. We will also return to this theme in Chapter Four, where we examine explicit rejections of empathetic understanding between protesters and university leaders as a special form of collusion.

CHAPTER TWO

Trigger warnings and vicarious engagement with trauma

Trigger warnings—written or spoken notifications attached to potentially sensitive materials in university settings—have been of particular interest in recent discussions of campus politics. It would be impossible to enumerate the types of materials that may be considered "triggering," for, as Jenny Jarvie notes, trigger warnings "have been applied to topics as diverse as sex, pregnancy, addiction, bullying, suicide, sizeism, ableism, homophobia, transphobia, slut shaming, victim-blaming, alcohol, blood, insects, small holes, and animals in wigs" (2014). Nevertheless, triggering items are most often considered to be depictions of hatred or violence directed at victims targeted by race, gender, or sexual identity. Over the past decade and a half, internet chatrooms, weblogs (blogs), and websites devoted to issues such as abuse, sexual assault, addiction, and self-harm have popularized the concept of the trauma trigger, initially borrowed from clinical literature on Post-Traumatic Stress Disorder (PTSD).

The interest in the trigger warning debate, however, is not entirely consistent with its salience on university campuses. Only a small number of universities require trigger warnings as a matter of policy, and, according to (non-scientific) polls and surveys such as the 2015 study conducted by the National Coalition Against Censorship, a similarly small percentage of faculty report that students have requested them. While such data should be interpreted with caution, they suggest that the debate about trigger warnings has received attention for reasons other than the impact of such notifications on teaching and learning in the classroom.

Similarly, while it is important to recognize that there *are* university students—although precisely how many remains unclear—who bring with them to the university a history of what has traditionally been understood as "traumatic experience" and the continued psychological distress associated with it, these students may not be those most actively involved in the trigger warning debate. For students who have suffered, for example, life-threatening accidents or acts of violence, sexual assault, debilitating physical injury, abuse, or exposure to military combat, traumatic experiences are "overwhelming and … exceed or greatly challenge the affected individual's capacity to cope" (Courtois et al., 2016). For such students, to say that classroom material "triggers" post-traumatic symptoms is to say that it generates extremely painful intrusive thoughts or memories, autonomic arousal, emotional dysregulation, episodes of derealization or depersonalization, and/or severe disruptions in attachment, self-care, and functioning.

Although it would seem reasonable to offer trigger warnings to such students in such cases, it is difficult, if not impossible, for instructors or administrators to know which students need trigger warnings and what specific words, ideas, or symbols will be triggering. Nevertheless, practical problems in applying trigger warnings do not necessarily refute the underlying premise that a well-placed caution may permit a student suffering acute post-traumatic symptoms to schedule an additional appointment with a therapist, or to hold a discussion with an instructor about how sensitivity to course material may affect in-class performance or other work.

Where the trigger warning debate becomes more complicated, and where we will focus our attention, is on cases where students' and others' equate their experiences with trauma (and with susceptibility to post-traumatic triggering) in an effort to give shape to less well-defined relationships and experiences in their inner worlds. That is, we are concerned with the meaning of the transposition of problematic internal object relations into protests and conflicts involving traumatizing and triggering external events and actors.

Over the past four decades, the category of trauma has been "opened up" to the point that the term is now applied to a wide range of experiences of pain, shock, suffering, deprivation, or victimization. The popularity of trauma language and the ascendency of trauma studies in numerous academic fields have been at least partly responsible for creating a discursive environment in which it is no longer surprising to hear even minimally stressful experiences named "traumas." Some of today's students, for example, express worry or anger that preparing a paper or leading an in-class discussion will be "traumatizing" for them. While graded writing and public speaking may be fearsome, and while these events may even have resonances with adverse experiences and anxieties, these claims strike us as clearly hyperbolic with respect to trauma.

Thus, a term originally meant to distinguish extreme experiences that pose existential threats (whether physical, emotional, or both) is being used far more broadly. This broader use of the language of trauma should not be considered free of political intent. That is, even those who may not be familiar with the work of Judith Herman may agree with her well-known assertion that every instance of traumatic injury "is a standing challenge to the rightness of the social order" (quoted in Shay, 1995, p. 3), and may find that appropriating the power of the term draws attention to a seriousness of claims of victimized persons or marginalized groups.

At the same time, the idea of experience, writ large, has been granted a privileged moral and epistemological status in recent years. The immense attention and weight given to trauma claims and trauma studies is inseparable from the premise that "lived experience"—specifically lived experience that is untranslatable into cognition and language—is true and real (or is 'the Real' for someone like Jacques Lacan). "Lived experience" has been (conspicuously) spared from modern and postmodern critiques of subjectivity and rationality and, as a result, seems to some to be the only remaining source of cultural authority (see Bowker, 2016). The impetus to set up "experience" as the sole reliable criterion of truth is, like attention to trauma, rooted in political as well as philosophical motives: The more we attend to difference (and *différance*), domination, and the subaltern, the more we mistrust reason and turn to testimonies, embodiments, and other expressions of the lived experiences of the oppressed.

Thus, Cathy Caruth, perhaps still the best-known trauma theorist in the humanities, teaches that traumatic memories are "literally" true (1996, p. 57), and remain "absolutely true to the event" that sponsored them. Intrusive thoughts, flashbacks, nightmares, and other symptoms of trauma compose, therefore, "not a pathology … of falsehood or displacement of meaning, but of history itself" (1995, p. 5). In other words, traumatic experience and the post-traumatic symptoms through which we come to know it are "absolutely" real and "literally" true. The agenda that drives Caruth's assertions is to turn trauma into a paradigm, to make of traumatic experience a way of understanding or experiencing all of life.

Caruth and those trauma theorists who share her views have suggested that we inhabit, or, rather, that we must envision ourselves as inhabiting, a post-traumatic era, a "post-traumatic century" (Felman, 1995, p. 13). One consequence of doing so is that we come to doubt the possibility that historical truth may be preserved in rational thought or expression and, instead, that we turn to fractured testimonies, affects and symptoms, and other artifacts to (re)constitute reality. Thus, we must "understand history [itself] as the history of trauma" (Caruth, 1996, p. 60), since "history," itself, "is precisely the way we are implicated in each other's traumas" (p. 24). We must even approach "history as holocaust" (Felman & Laub, 1992, p. 95), which is to say not that we should attend to this or that holocaust in our study of history, but, rather, that all of history *is* holocaust, that even our own personal histories may be, in this sense, holocausts, and that to understand what has happened or what is happening to us as individuals and communities, we must put ourselves in the place of one suffering or witnessing a holocaust.

At a minimum, such attitudes would seem to suggest that the reigning view of trauma, experience, and truth is one in which what we think of as reality is not determined by historical accounts, reasons, evidence, or the like, but, rather, by intuitions of terror, apocalyptic imaginations, identifications with victims, and intense emotional reactions. Walter Benjamin summarized this claim aptly when he wrote that "to articulate the past historically does not mean to recognize it in "the way it really was," but rather "to seize hold of a memory as it flashes up at a moment of danger" (2003, p. 391). What Benjamin, Caruth, Felman, and others are suggesting, and what has been accepted to a surprising degree in many university cultures, internet cultures, and popular cultures is that, *because* reality itself is constituted by pervasive yet ultimately unthinkable traumatization, only immediate experiences, memories that "flash[] up at a moment of danger," and visceral identifications with trauma victims lead us to the truth.

It is beyond the scope of this chapter to delve more deeply into the intellectual discourses and broader psycho-social dynamics that have created what may be called a "culture of trauma," or, as Fassin and Rechtman name it, an "empire of trauma" (2009). Instead, in this chapter, we focus on the phenomenon of vicarious identification with trauma in the university. To focus on vicarious identification with trauma (and not traumatized students alone) is not to suggest that traumatizing or re-traumatizing events are absent from university settings, nor to dismiss the seriousness of claims that certain encounters have been triggering for students or others. On the contrary, attending to the vicarious experience of trauma permits us to recognize that when university members invoke the concept of trauma, when they identify themselves with victims of trauma, and when other university members are cast in the role of (re-)traumatizing victimizers, something important is being expressed about the nature and quality of students' psychic lives. In this chapter, we strive to understand the meaning of these expressions.

Critical retaliations

Before we treat directly the nature of and reasoning behind requests for trigger warnings, it is important to take a moment to note the presence of a harsh critical reaction to such requests, a reaction that sheds light on the trigger warning debate and what it signifies. A number of cultural observers have cited calls for trigger warnings as evidence of the frailty of the millennial and post-millennial generations and of the indulgent attitude of contemporary learning institutions. Popular articles, such as "The coddling of the American mind" (Lukianoff & Haidt, 2015)— with echoes, of course, of Allan Bloom's *The Closing of the American Mind* (1987), which famously critiqued an earlier generation of university students—"Trigger Happy" (Jarvie, 2014), "Yale's idiot children" (Williamson, 2015), and "The 'Yale snowflakes': Who made these monsters?" (O'Neill, 2015) offer stinging judgments of students, families, and universities.

In some instances, the language employed in these articles is so caustic that it is difficult to avoid the conclusion that the author's intent is to subject his or her targets—again, most commonly, students—to shame and ridicule. For instance, in his article, "Campus special snowflakes melt upon contact with Greek mythology," John Hayward calls the advocacy for trigger warnings at Columbia University discussed below "totalitarian gobbledygook," while mocking a particular student as an ignorant child, "startled into a shivering neurotic heap and made to feel *physically unsafe* because the professor didn't warn her before dropping the Ovid bomb" (2015, emphasis in original).

Although to a lesser degree, prominent academic leaders have also been involved in the vocal rejection of trigger warnings. In 2014, the American Association of University Professors (AAUP) decried trigger warnings as a "threat to academic freedom." Likewise, John Ellison, Dean of Students at the University of Chicago, recently informed the incoming class of 2020—in what became a public and controversial letter—that the university's commitment to "academic freedom" meant that it would not tolerate demands for trigger warnings or safe spaces where students might "retreat from challenging ideas or perspectives." The assumption driving the AAUP's and Ellison's stance, that students who support trigger warnings intend to use them to shield themselves from "ideas and perspectives at odds with their own" (Ellison quoted in Vivanco & Rhodes, 2016), may do a disservice to the complexities of the trigger warning issue, since the most responsible advocates argue that trigger warnings permit students struggling with traumatic events to engage (and not to "retreat from") re-traumatizing (and not merely intellectually "challenging") material, in spite of the emotional discomfort it might cause.

In fact, dismissive criticisms of trigger warnings dovetail with pejorative and stigmatizing uses of the diagnosis of PTSD in ways that, perhaps ironically, lend support to the idea that traumatized students may benefit from trigger warnings. Harvard psychology professor Richard McNally, for instance, succinctly titled his editorial in the *New York Times*: "If you need a trigger warning, you need PTSD treatment" (2016). Although the aim of that article was to critique the idea of trigger warnings and to delegitimize students' expressions of need, McNally's argument may be taken to suggest that those who suffer from PTSD have a legitimate claim to accommodation, as do students with physical, psychological, or learning disabilities.

Similarly, with respect to the Columbia University case to be discussed presently, Elizabeth Nolan Brown has argued that "if the mere discussion of rape causes [a] student to feel panicked and physically unsafe—then she needs help treating severe post-traumatic stress disorder, not a fucking trigger warning. I say that with no judgment ..." (2015). Brown's assertion that "no judgment" is implied in her sardonic manner of questioning the student's distress and in her profanity-laden statement is, of course, absurd. And this absurdity brings us to an important initial problem in the debate about trigger warnings: hostility directed at students for suggesting they would benefit from trigger warnings.

Ironically, the idea of trigger warnings seems to "trigger" hateful responses among some critics and academic leaders, suggesting that the trigger warning debate is about more than trigger warnings: It is about questions of control and responsibility for the inner life of the student, about what the student must "learn" in the university, and about the various groups and roles (e.g., teachers and students, the powerful and the powerless, victims and victimizers, etc.) defined in the debate. Derogatory language aimed at students who support trigger warnings suggests that critics and authorities have been drawn into the drama of victimization and traumatization of university students, a drama in which they play a role marked by intolerance of expressions of need and hostile rejections of requests for care. Here, students who express need and ask the university for help are rebuked, are told to "toughen up"—often in the name of defending not students' but teachers' "academic freedom"—or are ridiculed as "idiot children" or "monsters." Such attributions and refusals may also be driven by a form of envy closely related to a hatred of students (see Bowker, 2016). This hatred likely has many sources, but one appears to be rage directed at students who dare to demand accommodations that others, perhaps the critics themselves, have been denied or, perhaps, have denied themselves.

This hostility mirrors and repeats, in some sense, the experience of being "triggered." That is, Dean Ellison's letter, the statement of the AAUP, and the disapproving if not simply nasty attacks on students in popular journalism, may be, or may appear to be, evidence of the need for trigger warnings, especially in the eyes of students. Students may feel unsafe if the organizations or communities to which they belong seem contemptuous of their requests for help, if requests for care are taken as proof of weakness, cowardice, or other shame-worthy qualities, or if their environments do not seem to be "safe" places to articulate their needs, not least because their expressions of need violate the "freedom" of their teachers. Students who request trigger warnings may experience, in having their requests ridiculed, a form of emotional assault, degradation, and abandonment. Harsh rejections and dismissals of students' expressions of need for protection, then, likely deepen students' vicarious identifications with trauma and with the traumatized.

It is also important to consider the possibility that it is this very identification—the identification between student and victim suggested by the request for trigger warnings—that lies at the root of critics' hostility toward trigger warnings and that provokes critics' aggressive language. Identifying with the victim *calls forth* victimizing behavior from others who perceive themselves to be cast in the role of victimizers. Provoking victimizing behavior from others is very much a part of the unconscious intent of identification with the victim, since continued victimizing behavior validates the identification. What is more, those who come to be identified with the victimizing role, even while enacting this role, may simultaneously resent being cast in this way and may become enraged or lash out at those who have cast them so.

Perhaps most importantly, since identifying with victims can support one's sense that one has the right to express disappointment, grief, or rage when one's needs are not met, others may experience envy of victims and those who identify with them. If one is, or identifies oneself as, a victim of trauma, one may enjoy a certain freedom from guilt about aggressive and destructive impulses, perhaps particularly if those impulses are directed at those who failed to hear and meet needs. If one is, or identifies as, a trauma victim, one need not feel bad about aggression aimed at others because those others are now cast as the real aggressors, and any destructive impulses or actions directed at them may be reframed as a defense of the victimized self or group. Thus, victimizers may victimize victims for their audacity in claiming the enviable mantle of victimhood.

Although hostility is often directed at victims and at those who identify with them, those cast in victimizing roles experience, at the same time, an ambivalent temptation to internalize this attribution, even if they have not actually victimized anyone. As discussed in the previous chapter, the internalization of the role of the victimizer relies not only on attractions to aggression and desired identifications with victimizers (since victimizers are imagined to be those who cannot be victimized), but on a complex and contradictory attempt to temper the negative moral judgments associated with the victimizing role by establishing counter-identifications or alliances with victims by taking on the blame.

This dynamic—evident in recent efforts of "privileged" persons and groups to take on guilt, even for crimes they have not committed—will be explored again in Chapter Four.

These reflections suggest that trigger warnings themselves are not central to the trigger warning debate. That is, merely warning students about the likelihood of encountering explicit material from classrooms would do little to resolve what lies at the heart of students' complaints—since, after all, young people today are exposed to more explicit, violent, and graphic images than perhaps any generation in human history. Instead, to understand the debate about trigger warnings and what it represents, we must understand the dynamics of victims and victimizers, as well as the way that the debate about triggering represents a debate about the extent to which universities should facilitate the usurpation of university spaces by group fantasies and social defenses, particularly those in which dramas of victimization and traumatization are mapped onto (what were once routine) university activities.

Triggering and groups

Perhaps the best-known recent case involving trigger warnings comes from Columbia University, where students enrolled in its core course, "Masterpieces of Western literature"—formerly named "Literature humanities" and still referred to by students as "Lit hum"—asked that instructors teaching Ovid's *Metamorphoses* warn students of the potentially triggering effects of Ovid's accounts of rape. An editorial in the student newspaper, *The Columbia Spectator*, read, in part:

> Ovid's "Metamorphoses" is a fixture of Lit Hum, but like so many texts in the Western canon, it contains triggering and offensive material that marginalizes student identities in the classroom. These texts, wrought with histories and narratives of exclusion and oppression, can be difficult to read and discuss as a survivor, a person of color, or a student from a low-income background. (Johnson, Lynch, Monroe, & Wang 2015)

Describing the experience of a particular student, the essay continued:

> During the week spent on Ovid's "Metamorphoses," the class was instructed to read the myths of Persephone and Daphne, both of

which include vivid depictions of rape and sexual assault. As a survivor of sexual assault, the student described being triggered while reading such detailed accounts of rape … However, the student said her professor focused on the beauty of the language and the splendor of the imagery when lecturing on the text. As a result, the student completely disengaged from the class discussion as a means of self-preservation. She did not feel safe in the class.

Let us first consider how the issue of a trigger warning is linked to identity, as it would seem that the demand for trigger warnings here arises less from the specific material designated to be distressing, and more from a clash between the norms of identity groups and those operating in the university space (the classroom) where the material was encountered. According to the essay, students' "identities" are "marginalize[d]" by the absence of trigger warnings in Lit hum courses. Their "identities" are understood primarily in terms of their membership in groups, most of which are said to involve significant experiences of "exclusion and oppression." Certain texts, the authors argue, are "difficult to read" if a student identifies as a survivor, as a person of color, or as a member of a low-income group. Experiences of "exclusion and oppression" are equated with traumas or traumatic stressors, since they are taken as grounds for offering (trauma-) trigger warnings to students affiliated with these (group) designations. We may be tempted to assume, then, that the demand for trigger warnings is essentially a demand that universities do more to recognize the "exclusion and oppression" students identify as an important part of their group identity and, therefore, as an important part of themselves.

But when we ask "Why, exactly, did the student described in the essay feel so unsafe that her survival (her "self-preservation") was threatened?," we arrive at a curious answer. While it is understandable that a student who had been sexually assaulted might feel that Ovid's text awakened memories and emotions associated with that experience, what seems truly to threaten the student is that the course group functioned in a way that was distinct from and even opposed to the student's need to protect herself from the anxiety and terror associated with recalling or re-experiencing her own sexual assault. While the course group read Ovid's myths as myths, the student read them as accounts of sexual assault, and, more specifically, as accounts of her own sexual assault. Indeed, the course group, by focusing on the "beauty" and "splendor" of the rape scenes, came to appear to the student as a sexual assaulter, perhaps even as her own sexual assaulter, reveling in the "beauty" and "splendor" of rape. Therefore, the course group became identified with a victimizing, assaultive force and the student felt endangered, threatened, "not … safe."

While the course group seems to have been experiencing a discussion of a historical and literary text, the student was likely experiencing something very different. The student seemed to seize "hold of a memory as it flashe[d] up at a moment of danger," but the course group did not. In this way, the course group did not experience reading and discussing Ovid as dangerous; it did not attend to the student's experience of danger; it did not attune itself to the student's experience; and it did not dedicate itself to the formation of moral judgments about the act of rape or express compassion for the victim. While the student was engaged with a depiction of trauma, the course group was engaged with the text but *dis*engaged from the trauma of rape. To be disengaged from the trauma of rape then made the course group appear, to the student, to be engaged with rape not as victims but as victimizers. To "preserve" herself amidst a group of victimizers, the student "disengaged" from the group.

While it is beyond the scope of this chapter to explore the many meanings of sexual assault, it is hard not to notice the theme of abandonment in the essay's description of the student's reaction. The student experienced the course group as having abandoned her in a way that may be reminiscent of the abandonment involved in sexual assault, which includes the "setting aside" of the subjectivity, will, and privacy of the victim, as well as the setting aside of the terror, pain, and fear she may experience, all in order to treat her as an object to be abused for gratification. For this student, feeling abandoned by the course group may have been as triggering, or even more triggering, than the experience of reading and discussing Ovid.

Of course, abandonment is not unique to situations involving sexual assault. Failures of attunement by parents are experienced by children as abandonments, as the (nascent) subjectivity, will, and privacy of the child is disrupted when a parent either neglects the child's needs or strives to control the child's emotions, thoughts, and behaviors. This situation frequently leaves children with weak psychic boundaries, unable to separate their inner world from the world outside, and unable to develop the internal capacities required to manage, moderate, and, to some extent, control internal experience. Abandonment, then, is associated with a loss of self-determination inasmuch as the self is thwarted in its attempts to be and know itself. Instead, the inner world of the child who is emotionally abandoned is chaotic in large part because the child is excessively dependent on others and on external stimuli in order to feel safe, alive, and connected, which is to say, to be anything but abandoned.

This dilemma may be repeated in the debate about trigger warnings, since the notion that a word, idea, or symbol can operate as a psychological trigger means that it provokes a powerful (internal) outcome. The individual who claims to be susceptible to triggering, even without reference to the stressors or traumas that may have made him susceptible, reveals his inner world's dependence on and vulnerability to external events. But it is not necessary that we take at face value the claim that it is a word, idea, or symbol that is always or often a trigger. What is likely to be more difficult to manage is the perception that one has been abandoned in a way that leaves one feeling out of control of one's self and one's inner experience. This loss of control, of course, is blamed on others, such that others are made to bear responsibility for internal emotional states and are blamed for having failed to protect the self from being triggered and (re-)traumatized.

Thus, the failure to find emotional attunement or resonance with others is likely to be more triggering than any particular material, because this failure of attunement is evocative not only of experiences of "exclusion and oppression" but of earlier abandonments in which the child's true needs were ignored. If such failures have been internalized as a sense of being surrounded by those who do not share one's experience and who, therefore, condemn it, one's inner world becomes, almost by definition, a dangerous place to be, a place where one's thoughts and emotions are not safe because their expression is likely to yield a critical response, a response that, in turn, generates shame. If the social defenses typically relied on by the student to block out shame are unavailable or insufficient in a classroom, then the pain of the experience of being triggered cannot be managed and the student may feel helpless and overwhelmed. This process likely contributes to the confusion between students' experiences of anxiety and those of re-traumatization, since trauma is associated with being helplessly overwhelmed by affect.

The possibility that students may feel abandoned, assaulted, or ashamed in university classrooms is closely related to an important difference between the nature of course groups and other types of groups with which students may be involved, such as groups of friends or family, identity-based or advocacy-based groups, and survivor or support groups. Students who belong, for instance, to survivor groups are likely to find in such groups reliable beliefs and fantasies about shared experiences of adversity that are far less likely to be reinforced in a classroom, unless, of course, the classroom is transformed by the instructor, the university, or the course group itself into a kind of survival-oriented group, an important possibility we consider below. In such groups, beliefs about the nature of the experiences members face or have faced, along with powerful judgments about these experiences and those responsible for them, are what hold the group together. Indeed, individuals who experience conflict *within* such groups—one such case will be discussed in the following chapter—find that they face great pressure to align their ideas, beliefs, and fantasies with those of the group, lest they be cast as traitors.

When shared experiences define a group's identity, group members find relief from certain forms of "exclusion and oppression" they may have known in the past, whether those be experiences in the family or in the broader society, or, most likely, a combination of the two. Inside the group, on the contrary, group members share something important and exclusive that determines their belonging. At a deeper level, however, when shared experiences (or fantasies of shared experiences) come to define a group's identity, this process affirms the damaging premise that the individual's identity, if it is to hold value, must be adapted to or aligned with the identities of others. In this way, the social defense associated with organizing groups around shared experience *reimposes* on group members adverse experiences of self-denigration. To belong to a group that requires an emotional abandonment of oneself, then, both protects the self from, and re-enacts the painful drama of, abandonment.

For this reason, part of the susceptibility to being triggered likely includes an unconscious awareness of the self's capacity to collude with the process of self-abandonment. Indeed, the recognition of the self's own participation in eroding its boundaries and permitting itself to be determined by external factors may be, in itself, a powerful trigger for negative judgments of the self and subsequent anxiety (see also Bowker, 2016). The fact that the individual has colluded, albeit in a coercive and impossible situation, in not being herself inspires guilt (for destructive impulses directed toward parental figures) and shame (for her neglected, diminished self).

Clearly, many forms of group-belonging involve a sort of bargain by which individuals repress aspects of self-experience that do not accord with the beliefs, assumptions, and fantasies of the group, and, in exchange, receive reliable investment in and support for their own (good) group identities. That is, failures of care, which might include forms of neglect, abuse, or denigration, that interfere with the child's development of self and identity may persuade the child to identify with groups whose identities are, themselves, defined by neglect, abuse, and denigration by outsiders. Such groups maintain their vitality by turning painful emotions outward and focusing their attention on external victimizers, whether those are taken to be certain specific individuals or groups or, more broadly, all those who do not meet the main criterion of group-membership: the sharing of the group's beliefs and fantasies about the sources of its emotional suffering. One finds in such groups an effort to blur the boundary between outsiders and victimizers such that those who are, for example, "privileged" by not having been victimized may be considered morally responsible for the victimization of those who have, since the privileged have enjoyed or continue to enjoy the condition of (presumed, fantasized) control and safety.

If a group member comes to hold even a neutral attitude on the question of the danger and culpability of outsiders, he may find that he disrupts a primary function of the group, which is to offer members an external environment that matches an inner fantasy, where the boundary of the group delineates good and bad, and where the self's identity is protected from inner and outer attack. By "inner and outer attack," we mean that the group protects its members not only from attacks from outsiders—for instance, that the group would likely rally around members exposed to derogatory or discriminatory treatment—but, perhaps more importantly, from doubt about the reality of their shared interpretation of experience. This means that the group protects its members from any awareness of an internal source of attack on the value of the self and of their collusion with the imposition of a denigrated identity. Belonging to the group reassures members that their rage at victimizers is morally justified because they are innocent victims, that their identities are sources of pride and not of shame, and that they (as a group) are different from and in certain respects superior to those who do not share their fantasy of their experience.

Thus, victimizing, privileged, or even indifferent characters in the external world come to represent figures in the inner reality of individuals and groups in part because of the need to disavow responsibility for violent impulses that now originate internally, however they may have been prompted originally by dysfunctions in early object relations. Seen in this light, preoccupation with trauma and identifications with trauma victims appear to be a way to externalize violent impulses while, at the same time, indulging them in shared fantasy. There is comfort in the idea that our suffering is entirely the result of events originating outside, in the violent acts of aggressors, just as there is tremendous hope in the fantasy that we can overcome our suffering by naming our aggressor(s) in re-enactments of our victimization that seem to offer clarity about who is good and who is evil (on naming the aggressor, see Bowker, 2017).

To say as much is certainly not to imply that individuals and groups have not experienced assault, exclusion, and oppression. But the student who feels triggered in a classroom where Ovid is studied feels triggered because—or to the extent that—the goal of a classroom discussion of Ovid is to understand Ovid, rather than to make moral judgments of Ovid's mythological characters. While there may be room for such judgments in university classrooms, traditional course groups are not primarily dedicated to the activity of solidifying moral judgments against persons, groups, or fictional characters. In fact, some university faculty consider it to be their duty to do the opposite: to "unsettle" or "problematize" moral judgments, so as to generate critical thinking or to prompt recognition of the limitations of our own moral orientations.

If it is not certain texts but certain course groups that are really triggering to students, then trigger warnings are directed at universities and university members *not* for being excessively judgmental, but for being *inadequately* judgmental. That is, the problem lies not in the fact that the classroom environment is insufficiently diverse so much as that it is excessively diverse: The course group is unsafe because it is not bound by a shared experience and so is unable to reassure its members that their internal reactions will be affirmed by others. For students who require other individuals and groups to share in their powerful emotions, judgments, and defenses in order to defend themselves against shame, the classroom is not a safe place to be. By the same token, if university classrooms come to be dedicated to the activity of solidifying moral judgments, then these classrooms will be, in many respects, safer and less triggering—but at the same time more coercive and less conducive to genuine intellectual development and students' self-determination—than those in which the primary goal is to think about, discuss, and understand the course material (see also Bowker & Fazioli, 2016). Insofar as the university-defined space known as the classroom establishes itself as a space devoted to understanding rather than shared experience and moral judgment, it becomes a dangerous place.

Ambivalences of triggering

We have argued that what is thought to be triggering or re-traumatizing about exposure to certain materials involving victimization, abuse, or "exclusion and oppression" is not primarily that these materials recall an individual's or group's traumatic history. On the contrary, what is triggering or re-traumatizing is that the material is presented in settings in which group identities defined by shared experience, group fantasies, and social defenses are not given pride of place. The subordination of the norms of the support group or survivor group to the norms of the university course group is taken to be an abandonment of those with painful histories. Such individuals find themselves in "dangerous places" when social defenses are ineffective.

Although the experience of being triggered repeats aspects of painful relationships and emotions, being triggered likely holds ambivalently invested attractions as well. Triggers may serve an important psychic function: Through the intensity of emotion they provoke, they may offer semblances of meaning and vitality to our lives. Here, we may find, as did Winnicott, that there is a powerful urge to stage manageable dramas or, as Winnicott calls them, "minute" traumas, in order to re-experience emotions of grief and hatred (1989, pp. 145–146).

In most university classrooms, there is an authority figure (an instructor) who is accused of triggering powerful emotions in a setting in which it is not safe to have them. So, in addition to the ambivalent desires of students, there may be instructors who assign, view, or read accounts of violence, rape, or torture for reasons having little to do with pedagogy. Indeed, there are likely to be instructors who use their power to abandon students to encounters with distressing materials in settings in which powerful emotional responses are not supported or permitted. Such activities represent attempts on the part of instructors to share in the fantasy life of students, to vicariously experience abandonment through them, and to engage in a kind of "virtual reality" relationship with them. This possibility also holds for dismissive and abusive verbal attacks by critics or academic authorities on those who advocate trigger warnings. These attacks are sometimes grounded in staunch defenses of instructors' "academic freedom," which may be taken to mean "freedom" to enact such dramas as a way of maintaining vitality in their own emotional and fantasy lives.

But even where this is not the intent of instructors, triggering materials, trigger warnings, and even the trigger warning debate itself serve as invitations to a shared fantasy experience. At a conscious level, engagement with graphic depictions of violence, especially against defenseless victims, encourages participants to bond together in moral judgment and condemnation of violence and to commit themselves to doing what they can to protect victims. In being triggered, we find access to the intense emotions that confirm our belonging to groups that confirm our identities as victims and others' identities as victimizers. That is, if a group shares real and/or fantasized experiences of "exclusion and oppression," then vicarious engagement with trauma fortifies a group member's sense of identity-achievement as a member of that traumatized group. Of course, at an unconscious level, identification with the victimizers is also attractive for reasons discussed in the previous section, including its use as an alternative strategy to overcome, in imagination, our own victimization. So far as this is the case, vicarious engagement with trauma sanctions both a conscious identification with victims and an unconscious identification with victimizers.

Individuals and groups come to depend on vicarious experiences of trauma—both being triggered and triggering others—to affirm group identities. Historical or fictional depictions of violence, rape, torture, or other kinds of victimization serve to represent, in the outside world, fantasy characters in internal dramas. When they do so, those historical and fictional depictions take on the special reality of psychic life. If fantasy is reality in the inner world, then victimization encountered in the external world serves as a representation of (inner) experiences of "exclusion and oppression." What is real for the individual or group is the presence of intense emotions of loss, grief, shame, and rage, even when the individual or group may not have suffered traumatic experiences such as torture, violence, or assault.

The possibility that depictions of victimization and trauma serve as representations in the external world of fantasies can help us understand the tendencies of those who call for trigger warnings to exaggerate or distort the degree of their suffering. Preoccupation with extreme violence and victimization highlights the disproportions intrinsic to early emotional experience, where figures in the inner world *are experienced* as larger than life, taking on extreme and often morally absolute (pure good and pure evil) qualities. It is this special intensity of emotional life experienced by a child at a time when the capacity to modulate emotions is poorly developed that links adverse experiences that may not be, strictly speaking, traumatic, to trauma. Identification with victims of trauma, then, is an expression of parental failure in helping the child develop her capacity to regulate her emotional responses. Because of this, parental abandonment, as we have suggested above, can be a uniquely powerful factor in fostering the special intensity of fantasies of victimization.

Another way of looking at the ambivalence of triggering is to consider the possibility that triggering reminds us of our identification with loss and of the motivations that drive us to seek membership in groups that serve as a replacements for the positive identifications and healthy attachments missing or lost in non-facilitative environments (on trauma as replacement, see Bowker, 2016). That is, whereas a nurturing and facilitative environment may be internalized as the foundation for the elaboration of a self-determined identity, experiences of abandonment or rejection may be internalized as a powerful impulse to adapt, with the result that the inner world becomes a dangerous place to be. In this case, while the inner world is filled with threat and anxiety, it is also a familiar place where the endangerment of the self is what feels real and where steps must be taken both to stave off annihilation and to hold onto the sense of danger associated with it.

If, in early life and in groups, we are forced to adapt to external demands, then our subsequent losses of self and self-boundaries become the grounds for an agonizing connection to fantasies of trauma. Here, what feels real is the experience of abandonment and the absence of relationships that facilitate self-contact and identity-development rooted in the presence of self. If such experiences are shared (or imagined to be shared) by a group, and if that group comes to form a central part of the individual's identity, then threats to the norms and fantasies of the group, in the form of triggering language or material, remind the individual that the loss of self he feels is also, paradoxically, "who he is." That is, if vicarious engagement with trauma has become a substitute for self-contact, and if group belonging has come to stand in for individual identity, the same early failures in facilitating and relating that threatened to destroy our selves are transposed into experiences that affirm our (group) identities, but only if we are able to project these failures onto suitable targets in the external world. If we are triggered by the words or actions of others, we reinforce the power of external victimizers in our own dramas of being abandoned and abandoning ourselves.

Of course, vicarious engagement with traumatic experience offers us the opportunity to identify emotionally damaging relationships with events that are more definitive in the damage they do to victims. Experiences of emotional non-attunement and sensations of losses of internal control and self-contact can be difficult to articulate. They may have been generated over years or decades through complex patterns of relating to parents, family members, or significant others. Vicariously experiencing trauma through more readily definable triggering material affords us a simpler yet partly obscured means of accessing our inner worlds. This is because, while the trauma is vivid and perhaps even tangible, our experience of it is vicarious, which allows us to keep it at a distance. Then, vicarious engagement with trauma becomes a defensive strategy for avoiding genuine engagement with our inner worlds.

Identifying neglectful or abusive relationships with traumatic events also protects an individual from awareness that her parents' failure to attend to her emotional struggles in a helpful way—as in emotional abandonment—was an important factor in provoking violent impulses and fantasies directed toward them. Such violent impulses and fantasies are threatening to the child not only because they are directed at good objects, but because the individual may feel shame and guilt if she takes responsibility for them in order to protect the parent. Once associated with a traumatic event, encounters with triggering material recall the abandonment and rejection of the child's nascent self, linking the anxiety of being triggered to the anxiety of the child who faces grief, shame, and self-hatred at a time too early to cope with them. A simpler narrative of trauma, where the victimizers are not good objects, offers individuals a way to avoid a significant amount of internal distress.

Part of the damage done by emotional abandonment involves the mystification of the child who must find in the abandoning figure a good object. That is, abandonment—which could include literal abandonment but need not—involves exposing the child too early to external demands, which, in turn, weakens his capacity to develop a healthy boundary between his inner world and the world outside, leaving him confused about what is "his" and what belongs to others. Paradoxically, the abandoning figure is frequently the object with whom the child most readily identifies. For this reason, emotional abandonment is among the most important factors in the abuse and exploitation of children. We can understand this if we can understand the parent's behavior as that of abandoning the duty to protect the child from the parent and from the parent's world of (adult) experiences, expectations, and demands.

Consider the most salient case, and the case most relevant to our reflections on the meaning of triggering: fantasies about sexual assault. For individuals of all genders, such fantasies may be present for a variety of reasons, including reasons other than actually having been involved in a sexual assault. Fantasies of sexual assault suggest the presence of a problematic relationship between desire and aggression, a relationship in which feelings of aggression directed toward desire's object makes desire itself seem to have a destructive end. When this is the case, the desire for an object and the wish to be a desired object cannot be fully divorced from impulses to victimize or be made a victim. If emotional abandonment is experienced by the child as a punishment for aggression, the child may come to associate aggression with the loss of desire's object. This can make the normal aggression associated with pursuit of desire's object feel dangerously destructive, which can lead to a powerful ambivalence about desire and sexuality and to the attachment of excessive guilt and shame to desire.

Sexual encounters in which the inner worlds of participants are dominated by an excess of aggression associated with desire can become assault-like or rape-like enactments. This observation is not intended to challenge the veracity of claims concerning sexual assault or to diminish in any way the problem of sexual assault on university campuses. Instead, we wish to consider the possibility that even if a sexual encounter is mutually consensual by outer (communal, legal) standards, one or both participants may experience the encounter as an assault in a way that is very real in the inner world. Individuals who have experienced sexual encounters in this way may not be fully aware of precisely why they feel violated, exploited, ashamed, or enraged by their experience, but may find that they identify with graphic depictions of sexual assault often classified as triggering, depictions in which a sexual encounter is clearly non-consensual. Such depictions give form and clarity to an ill-defined inner experience while also suggesting to the individual appropriate outlets for powerful emotions.

"Carry that weight"

As a final example of some of the complexities, group dynamics, and ambivalences of triggering, it will be helpful to consider another well-known instance of vicarious engagement with trauma, one for which no trigger warnings were requested or offered. In 2015, at Columbia University, the same university where students requested trigger warnings be attached to Ovid, an undergraduate student famously carried her mattress with her at all times during her senior year. She did so as part of a performance art project, entitled "Carry that weight," intended, in part, to protest the inadequacy of the university's response to her accusation of sexual assault against a male student two years earlier.

Taken as emotional communication, her performance might be construed as an effort to share with and provoke in others her feeling of having been violated. For this woman, her bed, and what it symbolized, became a space over which she had lost control, and, in response, she made her bed a public object. In this sense, as a result of her alleged assault and the lack of consequences for the accused party, her protest might be taken to express her loss of control over something deeply private and intimate: not only her bed but also her body, her privacy, her safety, and perhaps even her self.

In naming her performance "Carry that weight"—in the imperative mood—she implied that she was tasked with carrying the burden of her rape due to the failure of the university to punish her alleged attacker. But, since she carried her mattress to her classes and university functions, and since an important part of her performance involved accepting assistance from others in carrying her mattress, other university members became implicated in this emotional and physical demand. That her burden became a shared burden, and that her victimization became, in this sense, a shared victimization were also, therefore, important parts of the meaning of her performance.

This student's performance was, inarguably, exhibitionist. To say as much is not to judge its merits, only to remark that she was uncovering something intimate about herself, and that this uncovering was likely to inspire in others powerful emotional reactions, which might include compassion, sadness, guilt, shame, rage, even hatred. Similarly, it would be naive not to imagine that her exhibition was likely to provoke sexual fantasies about her as well as powerful internal reactions to those sexual fantasies. What this means is that her performance was likely to provoke in others intense emotions and moral judgments, along with moral judgments associated with the provocation of intense emotions.

It is not necessarily the case, however, that the kinds of emotional responses and moral judgments she sought were one-sided. That is, her performance may have been intended (consciously and unconsciously) to inspire at least two reactions, both equally important. First, we know that many who witnessed her protest took part in it by helping her "carry that weight" around campus. These individuals may have felt sympathy for her or anger about her victimization; they may have identified with her suffering, or offered implicit or explicit moral condemnations of her alleged attacker and the allegedly complicit university. In this respect, the performance recruited others into sharing a fantasy about victimization and shame: that by voluntarily participating in a re-enactment of a boundary violation, one may cast off the guilt and shame of the victim and displace it onto the victimizer. By publically re-enacting experiences of trauma or victimization, that is, some seek to take control of or master an experience that involved a loss of control in the inner world. This taking of control also involves condemning external agents who stand in for internal objects associated with denigrations of identity, while fending off guilt and shame for the aggression associated with condemnation by occupying the role of the innocent victim.

At the same time, a second sort of moral judgment—one not inconsistent with the first—surely entered into play. In a way, this student invited the university community into her bed. This representation of a boundary violation repeated, elongated, and, in one sense, magnified her own experience, as many forms of protest and performance art are known to do. In this case, however, the victim also played the role of victimizer, as bystanders who may have had no knowledge of or involvement with the situation found themselves sitting at a desk next to a young woman's mattress. While this experience in no way compares to the horror of sexual assault, this intrusion of an intimate object into what might be expected to be a public space might be judged by some as inappropriately provocative.

Thus, this student's performance was likely to provoke (some degree of) aggression directed *at her*, aggression not identical to, but reminiscent of, the aggression in acts of sexual assault. Others' aggression may have been provoked by having been seemingly "invited" into her bed, a bed that simultaneously represented a crime scene: a place where another's unwanted presence suggests sexual assault. Therefore, others were cast as, identified with, or associated with an alleged sexual victimizer. If part of the unconscious aim of the performance was to elicit not just compassion but to be the object of aggression and hate, then we might imagine that reliving such aggression and hate, perhaps even reliving the shame induced by being the target of aggression and hate, may have been a way of re-enacting the alleged assault.

In saying this, we are not attempting to judge this student, her performance, or the veracity or importance of her allegations of sexual assault. Rather, we seek only to explore the different intentions embedded in her performance. On one hand, the performance seems to say that the artist has been burdened by her experience of rape, and that she wishes others to know, see, feel, and even share in her victimization and its toll on her, expressed as continued, arduous labor. To imagine that this burden was imposed by her alleged attacker but would remain hidden if she, in her protest, did not make it visible or manifest is reminiscent of the posting of segregation-era signs by the art student discussed in Chapter One. Although, technically, she "chooses" to "carry that weight," the meaning of the performance is to testify to her lack of choice, to bear witness to the agony of having one's choice, will, and self-determination taken away.

While retaining her identity as victim, the student's performance also enacts the role of victimizer, just as others are forced to confront her experience of victimization as both victims (of her act, and via identification with her) and victimizers (of her, by being figuratively "forced" into her bed and by the implication in the act that all in the community share the burden of responsibility for her assault). To find oneself pressed up against a woman's mattress in a university corridor or classroom is a shocking experience, as it is intended to be. The experience is meant to be reminiscent of, but not identical to, this student's reported experience of being pressed against her own mattress and sexually assaulted in her bedroom. In this way, her act of protest may be considered deliberately triggering for others and even for herself. Even those who may not have experienced sexual assault, but whose fantasies are dominated by victimizing figures and by close associations between desire and aggression, may have found in her performance a powerful representation of aspects of their own fantasy lives.

Thus, as this student carried a part of her intimate, private world onto the university campus each day, she both discovered and created each day a new world of potential victims and victimizers. In doing so, she established a space around her where powerful (and ambivalent) emotions and extreme moral judgments were certain to emerge. The deliberate creation of a space where intense emotions and moral judgments predominate may seem surprising if we recall that such emotions and judgments often exert considerable psychological pressure and may even evoke memories of experiences in which the self was judged unforgivingly and subjected to shame or hatred.

We see in these two events at Columbia University—the reading of Ovid in a classroom and the carrying of a mattress around campus— that the perceived danger of triggers is correlated not only with the presence of provocative or explicit material but with emotional experience in an atmosphere in which shared moral judgment is unreliable, uncertain, or absent. Thus, whether comforting or victimizing others, the student may have found she was successful in her real goal: to bring the university community together as a group in a collective condemnation of sexual assault, of her alleged attacker, and of what they represent in her inner world.

CHAPTER THREE

Safe spaces and free speech

The debate over trigger warnings shares an important quality with the demand, articulated primarily by students and student groups, for "safe spaces" on university campuses: areas protected from putatively harmful or traumatizing speech. Both express a difficulty in contending with words and ideas we do not wish to entertain, which implies a struggle to maintain psychic boundaries and to "limit access" to our inner worlds (Levine, 2003, p. 61). If words, ideas, or symbols introduced by others have undue access to the inner spaces of the self, then efforts to impose restrictions on others' speech or conduct should not be surprising. As suggested in the previous chapter, experiences of being triggered or made to feel unsafe are best understood not as acute states brought on directly by the expression of specific words or ideas, but as reflections of a predicament in which others hold excessive sway over our senses of self and our identities, over who we are and who we take ourselves to be.

In such a condition, we are (or must be) who we are known to be by others. The loss of self-contact and subjective control implied by this situation, the precarious state of the individual, and the emotions associated with this loss and this state—including rage, grief, and hatred—are projected onto an external world perceived to be cruel and persecutory. A vulnerable individual living in a dangerous, victimizing world would seem to require a good deal of compassion, care, and protection from the outside, from the organizations to which he belongs, and from the broader society and cultures in which he takes part. Of course, this drama of victimization may hold force even if external victimizing forces are not present, and, instead, the most destructive impulses lie within. It is important to remember that the need to be safe *to be* oneself always bears a complex relation to the need to be kept safe *from* oneself.

The promotion of "safe spaces" on university campuses in the US and UK has meant, in some cases, the construction of literal spaces where restrictions on speech and conduct apply, areas on campus where certain words or ideas are forbidden, where one is "safe" from critical, judgmental, or "problematic" speech. The relationship between safe spaces and free spaces, which were once thought to be "safe" precisely because they were free from restriction, is now one of opposition. Free spaces are those in which speech and conduct (within the law and within reason) are tolerated. Thus, expectations of safety, when "safety" means protection from controversial or potentially offensive ideas or gestures, are forsaken upon entry. The University of California at Santa Barbara (UCSB), for example, has created two areas on its campus known as "free speech zones," where individuals and groups may speak freely without fear of being silenced by other university members based on the content of their speech (Garshfield, 2015).

There is a sense in which most, if not all, of the current conflicts in universities are conflicts over the meaning, extent, and relevance of the norm of free and open expression. Expression can take many forms, ranging from the written or spoken word to visual art, from musical performance to the way we dress. Among these, freedom of speech has been, and continues to be, at the center of controversy. (The term "freedom of speech" is used here to cover not only speech in the narrow sense, but the broader class of activities suggested by the term "expression.") As important as freedom of speech may be in the university, it should be borne in mind that the university is not a truly public space in which the norm of free speech (as it exists outside the university) applies. The difference is that, in the university, it is appropriate to insist that speech be consistent with the mission of teaching and learning, a limitation that does not apply elsewhere. Still, that mission, at least as it has been most commonly understood, calls for a significant measure of free expression, even if the boundaries of freedom in universities are not identical to those protected by civil and political rights outside.

Vulnerability and aggression

A typical instance of the struggle over freedom of speech in the university involves protest against an invitation extended to an individual to come to campus to speak on a sensitive issue, as in the case of Germaine Greer, who was "disinvited" from a speaking engagement at Cardiff University due to her position on gender-transitioning. Greer claims that sexual re-assignment surgery is more akin to self-violence than gender-change, that, in her words, "just because you lop off your penis … it doesn't make you a woman" (quoted in Clark-Billings, 2015). Greer's position, whatever its faults or merits may be, represents what, at least since Simone de Beauvoir's classic, *The Second Sex* (1949), and even well before it, has been considered a relatively mainstream contention that sex is distinct from gender, just as being female is distinct from being a woman. Part of Greer's argument is that becoming a woman is a complex and lengthy process involving socialization, interaction, and performance that cannot be simply transplanted via anatomical surgery.

Cardiff students claimed that Greer's presence on campus would cause "mental damage" to students who felt differently about transgender issues, particularly students who identify as transgender, and that the university could not, therefore, responsibly permit her to speak. Students engaged with the issue knew about Greer and what she was likely to say. They knew that she was not "one of them" and would not speak in a way consistent with being one of them. For those who called for denying her venue, speech that is not approved by the group of those "like us" is an act of aggression intended to do harm. In other words, for these students, a speaker who is unlike us and unwilling to speak in the approved way is, by definition, engaged in *hate speech*. Some believe that certain words can only be spoken by those in their group, and that certain issues should only be addressed by those in their group. Thus, objections have been raised to speakers who differ from those who feel most directly implicated by a sensitive issue, as in the recent disinvitation of male participants from a debate about abortion at Oxford University (O'Neill, 2015). Any failure on the part of the university to control what is said, the language used to say it, and even the identities of those who speak is considered an invitation to hate speech. This means that freedom of speech authorizes hate.

The issue of hate speech has been central in campus controversies about freedom of expression. Thus, the University of California at Santa Barbara (UCSB) made national news when a professor assaulted a pro-life student and confiscated her poster, which contained graphic images of what were described as "late-term abortions" (Volokh, 2014). All of this took place in UCSB's primary "free speech zone." Both administrative and criminal investigations ensued, and the professor was convicted of theft, battery, and vandalism. In her initial statement to police, the professor's first line of defense was that she "felt triggered by the images on the posters" (UCSB Police Department, 2014; see also Hayden, 2014b). Since she was "triggered in a negative way," the professor concluded that she had the right to forcibly remove the images from the free speech area. "Because the poster was upsetting to her and her students," the police report reads, the professor believed that "the activists did not have the right to be there." According to police, the professor carried the poster back to her office, which she describes "as a 'safe space,'" where she and her students destroyed it with a pair of scissors.

Interestingly enough, the majority of public (and university) support went not to the student exercising free speech in an area protected by the university, but to the professor. Letters written and statements given on her behalf argued that the anti-abortion group's words and images constituted "hate speech" and agreed with an initial statement made by the professor that the student-protestors were "terrorist[s]." Many agreed with the professor's claims that her actions were taken "in defense of her students and her own safety" and that the anti-abortion group's demonstration had "violated" her "personal right to go to work and not be in harm" (Volokh, 2014). Other statements of support claimed that the professor was "the victim of a media campaign to portray her as 'an Angry Black Woman,'" while her "seemingly happy demeanor" was merely the result of the fact that she is "'wearing the mask,' that is, she is hiding her actual state through a strategy of self-presentation that is a cultural legacy of slavery" (quoted in Turley, 2014; see also Hayden, 2014a).

For those who defended this professor's actions, what characterizes a "safe space" is the assurance that those in the space share, if not a common race or gender, specific attitudes and beliefs. What is "safe" about a safe space, then, is that it provides those who occupy it with a form of protection associated with belonging to a group. The group's identity, experience, and predominant fantasies are infused into the space, as it were. The group, then, may regulate the thought, speech, and conduct governing the space, and, in this way, may protect those in it from doubt, challenge, or contravention. Some, like the professor cited above, even maintain that this feeling of safety is akin to a fundamental "personal right." This assertion is rooted in influential emotional experiences and relationships discussed more fully below, as well as a lack of understanding of the particular (i.e., non-universal) nature of group norms. For now, we may say that if it is believed that feelings of "safety," understood in the sense described above, should be available to all persons, at all times, then conflict is inevitable, for any feelings of danger may be construed as rights-violations for which others may be held accountable. Others' expressions will be interpreted as forms of assault and may be labeled "triggering," "terrorist[ic]," or otherwise intolerable. Not surprisingly, aggressive responses to such speech will be countenanced as acts of "self defense."

Central to controversies concerning speech and safety in universities, then, is the impulse to experience the use of words as an act of aggression; and, given the intensity of the response in the example cited above, we may assume that this experience of the use of words and images, and the resulting association of free speech with hate, has substantial psychic validity. Regardless of whether it is legitimate to limit free speech in the way demanded by some students and faculty— and doing so would render speech on campus something less than "free"—the psychic equation of free speech with aggression carries considerable weight. Indeed, the link between speech and aggression is deeply embedded in the psyches of those driven to control use of language.

The experience of speech as assault begins with the emotional meaning that has been invested in the words used. In the case of Germaine Greer and transgender students, these are words that refer to gender difference. It is not surprising that these words would create discomfort or anxiety, given that the issues in question represent the complexity and ambivalence many people feel about their gender identities. Yet, transgender students have likely experienced the use of these words in a distinctive way, which is to say that the terms used to refer to gender, have, during these students' childhoods, likely provoked confusion, ambivalence, and anger.

It needs to be emphasized that the earlier in emotional development this experience occurs, the more it is *the words* that are at stake, and the less it is any complex idea of gender represented by words that causes problems. The distinction between words and ideas is important because the less an articulated idea of gender is in play, the more power is invested in words themselves. In the absence of an idea about gender, all we have to go on is the words and the emotional charge—"good" or "bad"—attached to them. When words carry the valences of good and bad, they establish a powerful link between identity (who we are) and our worthiness for love. This link between identity and worthiness raises the stakes in conflicts about language, because those conflicts become struggles over our ability to make a positive emotional investment in ourselves, in our ability to see ourselves as worthy. Under these conditions, words do not help us understand the complex realities of gender, they simply tell us whether our gender identification is good or bad. By contrast, the more we have access to complex ideas, the greater the possibility that we can move from good or bad judgments of self and other to an understanding that is free of moral judgment.

When words are used to tell us who we are and whether we are good or bad, they act as vehicles for external determinations of what is most important about us. The more our identity and sense of self are shaped, early in life, by how others know us and what they know about us, the more susceptible we are, later in life, to taking in the words others speak about us and to experiencing these words as determinants of who we are and how we feel about ourselves. And, the more susceptible we are to taking in the valences of the words spoken about us, the more powerful our need to find ways to control what others say. This means that the experience of speech as an assault has deep roots that involve the link between the development of identity and the demand for adaptation to external expectations.

While vulnerability to the words used by others may be inevitable in early emotional development, it does not follow that we must continue, throughout life, to cede power to outside authorities to determine our internal states of mind. On the contrary, the idea of maturation includes the expectation that we will develop internal resources needed to reduce, if not altogether eliminate, our vulnerability to external assessment. But this movement from vulnerability toward self-determination, from permeable self-boundaries toward a well-defined self, may be blocked and, as a result, vulnerability can persist as a quality of personality throughout life. The more vulnerable we are to assessments offered by or attributed to others, the more speech will provoke conflict.

As we have already noted, much depends on whether significant figures in our lives exploit our early vulnerability to the imposition or ascription of identity or, instead, respect the presence in us of a capacity for internal, or self-, determination. The attempt to impose an identity on a child that serves the emotional needs of parents, teachers, or other significant figures suppresses the child's aspiration to make identity reflect self-development, replacing that aspiration with an impulse to adapt to the needs of others. The more we adapt to others, the less we exist in our own right and the more we exist only as we are seen in the eyes of others.

It is important to emphasize that this non-existence in our own right manifests itself on two levels: the external and the internal. As an external matter, it leads to excessive vulnerability to and dependence on the judgments of others, expressed in the words they speak about us or the other forms of expression they use in communicating with us. As an internal matter, it is reflected in the way we take in the self-state provoked by the valence of the words and expressions used by others, and in the way these others become parts of our inner worlds. This internalization takes the form of a persistent internal (or fantasy) dialogue through which the struggle over control exerted by those outside comes to dominate our innermost thoughts.

The result of internalization is that our true self, having been excluded from our relationships with others, now finds itself under *internal* assault. Dominance in the inner world of fantasies involving a relentless attack on thoughts and actions that emanate from the self leads to a tendency to interpret others' speech about us as assault. In other words, once the struggle over adaptation has been internalized, the prohibition against thinking our thoughts becomes our own harsh judgment of our own impulse to express a way of being shaped by self-determination. An external world that is an unsafe place for self-expression becomes an inner world that is also an unsafe place for self-expression, an inner world in which we silence ourselves because it is unsafe to speak, hear, and know ourselves.

In this dangerous inner world, thinking our thoughts provokes harsh judgments of ourselves so that, to protect ourselves from the feelings of guilt and shame associated with forbidden thoughts, much that is important about us remains unthought, in other words, repressed. This internal repression of prohibited thoughts plays a vital part in fueling our struggle in the world outside over freedom of expression, since the more effective the repression of thoughts, the less we experience our own inability to think about them. When thoughts are repressed, we experience not a prohibition but an absence of prohibited thoughts. What cannot be thought cannot be experienced as unavailable to being thought.

Yet, it can also be said that the intensity of our need to prevent others from having certain thoughts offers evidence of the power that prohibits us from thinking them ourselves. That is, our prohibited thoughts manifest themselves in enactments of prohibitions against thinking featured in our relations with others, relations whose purpose is to prohibit them from thinking their thoughts. When this is the case, it is the (outer) enactment that provides evidence of the (internal) prohibition. Essential to this enactment is the repression of thought, carried out by silencing those outside who might speak forbidden words and express forbidden thoughts. When this strategy dominates, freedom of speech becomes considerably less important than the pursuit of a "safe space" governed by control over what is said and by whom it can be said.

Two kinds of freedom

To return to the initial example of this chapter, we might imagine that Germaine Greer hears transgender students saying that it is possible to be a woman without having undergone the experiences Greer considers to be the unique and enduring possessions of a woman. On the other side, transgender students hear Germaine Greer saying they are not women, thereby echoing a damaging message they may have heard throughout their lives. Greer's words, then, are heard as attempts to impose external judgments on transgender students that are radically inconsistent with what they know to be true about themselves. Greer, therefore, comes to represent the external source or container for what has likely become an internal voice that has told transgender students, or still tells them, that their identification with women indicates that there is something wrong with them.

As we have indicated, vulnerability to the words spoken by people like Greer should not be taken for granted, but should be understood as an expression of the degree to which those words fit themselves into the kinds of internal dialogues that give them power to provoke feelings of anger and shame. This combination of vulnerability, on one side, and aggression, on the other, is important in shaping conflicts over freedom and safety and therefore in thinking about how best to manage such conflicts.

Thus, we might say that, under the conditions outlined here, there are *two kinds of freedom*, both potentially connected to speech. The first links freedom of speech to the freedom to use speech to impose an alien identity and, in that act, to denigrate what is real and true about us. This is freedom of speech as license to assault. The second is the freedom to be able not just to speak, but to think, our thoughts. The second kind of freedom links freedom of speech to the freedom from harshly imposed internal prohibitions on our thoughts, which often take the form of assaultive internal dialogues with an internal authority. This kind of freedom is freedom of speech and thought as an internal matter: the freedom to speak freely about oneself to oneself.

The less the individual finds the inner world a place of refuge where it is possible to think about words, connect them to ideas, and assess their validity, the less secure her emotional attachment to the norm of freedom of speech and expression in the world outside. The result is that many individuals experience their inner worlds in ways that pose a serious challenge to one of the central ideals of the university. It needs to be understood that this challenge arises not out of the kind of willful disregard for liberal ideals we may be tempted to understand it to be, but out of personal experiences deeply embedded in the individual's psyche, experiences in which speech about identity by anyone who does not share that identity is equivalent to assault.

Conversely, the less powerful the internal prohibition against thinking, the more freedom of expression in the world outside connects to positively invested internal experiences, and the more committed we become to sharing with others the internal freedom that has become one of our most valued possessions. Thus, to understand the complexities of conflicts over "freedom" and "safety" when applied to speech, we must attend to what kinds of emotional preconditions must be met for individuals to break the equation of speech with assault and to be able to tolerate, and even welcome, free expression.

Group dynamics and thought control

Freedom of expression takes on significance for us to the degree that it connects with the internal freedom to think our thoughts. Therefore, the danger that the university will collude with students in prohibiting the expression of thoughts is that doing so will reinforce internal prohibitions against students *thinking their thoughts*. By colluding with students in the effort to ban expression, the university aligns itself with students' punitive internal impulses, bent on preventing free and open dialogue, whether internal or external. In other words, it is not simply restrictions on others that are enforced by the university when it colludes in limiting freedom of expression; it is the restrictive internal factor in all students that is reinforced by university authority.

Even where the words of others do not place an intolerable emotional burden on students, insisting that they do can be used as a strategy for taking control of others and finding gratification in the loss of freedom imposed on them. In other words, while students may well feel vulnerable, they may exaggerate their vulnerability as a strategy for casting others in the role of harsh and damaging critics and themselves in the role of innocent victims. Doing so may be as important as, or even more important than, protecting themselves from perceived danger. By shifting the source of danger away from the inner world, harmful intent is located in those outside who would express forbidden thoughts, while those engaged in the aggressive effort to control these others are protected from guilt and responsibility for their own destructive impulses. In this case, Sarah Ditum would be correct in noting how movements to deny venue and restrict speech such as "no platform" use "the pretext of opposing hate speech to justify outrageously dehumanising language," by naming speakers racist, abusive, or dangerous, while "set[ting] up an ideal of 'safe spaces' within which certain individuals [the speakers] can be harassed" (2014). Here, a "tool" once used to protect free speech and thought has "become a weapon."

Does this mean that the university should adhere to a policy of unrestricted freedom of expression? From what we have said so far, it should be clear that the matter is not so simple. This is because of the possibility that freedom of speech will authorize the repression of the thinking process and the suppression of prohibited thoughts. In other words, it is important to consider the "free speech" of the parent or authority figure who uses words to create an alien identity within the developing individual. While free speech can mean the freedom to think our thoughts, it can also mean the freedom of others to undermine our ability to do so.

Let us consider, again, the matter of Germaine Greer's invitation to speak on campus. It could be argued, in favor of inviting her, that a discussion of the nature of what it means to be a woman might reasonably include the presentation of the position that you are not a woman unless you have lived the life of a woman, or that you can only be a woman if you are born anatomically female. Those who articulate these positions are not necessarily engaged in hate speech; but they may be. Whether it is hate speech depends not only on the idea articulated but on the emotional intent of the communication. Here, it is worth noting that, in Greer's past engagements on the issue, she used clearly assaultive language in what may be interpreted as an attempt to prevent others from thinking thoughts unacceptable (to her) about what it means to be a woman. Thus, Greer at one point suggested that Caitlyn Jenner's transition to being a woman was a media ploy designed to promote a television show, offering ad hominem argument rather than reason or evidence in support of her position.

To refuse Greer the opportunity to speak would be to refuse her the opportunity to use derisive and provocative language to prevent others from thinking a thought she considers unacceptable: the thought that someone anatomically male could decide that he is, or can become, a woman; or that the kind of anatomical alteration she associates with self-violence could be decisive in determining gender. It is *not* inherently hateful to take the position that students who are or were anatomically male but who identify as women are not women, even though it may cause discomfort and anger in those who hear her speak. But using language to mock or belittle students who were not born female but who identify as women may reasonably be considered hate speech *if* its intent is to provoke anger and shame.

Clearly, Greer's intent, in several of her engagements, has not been to create an atmosphere appropriate to the process of thinking. And, in fairness, perhaps Greer did not consider this to be her primary responsibility. But by using language that raises the (moral) stakes and provokes powerful emotional responses, she has created an intensity of emotion inconsistent with thinking. By refusing Greer the opportunity to speak, the university might be seeking not to limit but to protect freedom of thought in the sense considered here, and, in that way, to protect the *internal* capacity for freedom of thought and expression without which the norm of free speech becomes empty. That is one possibility. Another possibility, of course, is that the university, in refusing her an invitation, is taking sides in a power struggle over who may speak and who may think about certain issues, in order to prevent others from thinking the unacceptable.

It follows that the university, in dealing with the matter of free speech, faces a real dilemma. So far as Greer's purpose is to control the words used by students to describe their gender, she stands in the role of the adjudicator of identity and of the words used to describe, indeed to create, identity. And so far as students who would prevent her from speaking seek to control her use of words, their struggle with Greer is a struggle over who will occupy the role of parents who adjudicate what children are allowed to know about themselves. Alternatively, so far as Greer is attempting to articulate and defend, through reasoned argument, a position about what it means to be a woman that differs from the meaning insisted on by transgender students, she is inviting dialogue rather than inciting a struggle over power.

The power struggle to which we refer is a struggle between groups, and, perhaps more specifically, between group identities. The group holds considerable power in controlling what thoughts are available to its members. On this matter, we would like to refer to an experience one of us had while teaching a course on hatred and group conflict, summarized in the following vignette:

> For perhaps ten years, I taught a course in group and organizational dynamics as part of an academic program in international administration. The main emphasis of that course was on "reflective autonomy in groups," which refers to the exercise of the capacity of the group member to remove herself emotionally from the group while still in the group so that she might observe the group in a more objective way and understand what is happening in it. A student who had taken a special interest in that class decided the following term to enroll in another course of mine on hatred and group conflict. That course was scheduled each year in the fall and therefore happened to coincide with Columbus Day, a day of celebration of Christopher Columbus, especially on the part of the Italian-American community, involving an annual parade. Over the years, the Columbus Day Parade had become an increasingly contentious event involving a counter-demonstration by members of the Native American community, who were outraged at the idea of celebrating an historical figure they associated with genocide. Emotions ran high.
>
> The week before the demonstration, the student brought in leaflets from the organizing committee of the protest against the

parade that contained some more or less incendiary rhetoric about the event. As I then discovered, this student had worked closely for several years with one of the leaders of the protest against the parade, someone who had been her mentor in college and a very important person in her life. I was concerned and somewhat disappointed that my student would bring this literature to class without comment on how it might be involved with some of the issues we were exploring there, but I offered no remark on the leaflets, as it was my policy to allow time for announcements of events on campus and to do so without comment.

A week after the parade and demonstration ensued, my student appeared on her own initiative in my office to discuss her experience. The leader of the protest against the parade had given a speech, parts of which I had seen on the television news. During that speech, my student told me she attempted to exercise the capacity for reflective autonomy by taking herself out of the protest group of which she was a member and listening to the leader's speech as if she were not a group member. When she did this, her reaction changed radically, in that what she heard now sounded very different than it had before. She told me that it now sounded to her like hate speech. I told her that it sounded that way to me as well.

She then proceeded to recount her experience the day of the protest. While at the protest, she found herself, with her mentor and a small group, on her way to what presumably was intended to be an act of civil disobedience, one that was risky in that, at the least, it would likely involve her getting arrested. As they walked to the planned site of the civil disobedience, the leader of the group stopped them and told them that they were about to take some risks and that this was the moment for those who wished to turn back to do so. My student thought for a moment, and then, alone among the members of the group, turned around and walked away.

We offer no judgment on this student's decision to walk away. We remark only that it seemed to express an internal process that freed her to think a previously unthinkable thought: the thought that the group to which she belonged exhibited qualities we associate with hate groups. This freedom is important, although it can only take the student so far. It is the beginning, and not the end, of an internal process. Beyond the exercise of reflective autonomy in groups, there is also the matter of an internal process that would enable the student to think about and understand the factors that drove her to associate herself with a group of this kind in the first place. Still, the exercise of reflective autonomy can make the next step a possibility, a possibility precluded so long as the student remains in the group in a way that means giving up on thinking about the group. Exercising reflective autonomy means thinking the thoughts that are prohibited by the group.

As we have suggested, claims about the intolerable suffering caused by uses of language are less often a reflection of actual suffering caused by free speech and more often a means of expressing and enacting group solidarity. To demand control over words and thoughts is to experience the power of the group over those outside the group *and* over its own members. Doing so establishes the dominance of the group over other groups, the dominance of members of the group over members of other groups, and even the dominance of the group over the individual group member.

That is, expressions and enactments of group solidarity challenge freedom of expression not only because of the way they foster powerful impulses to control what those outside the group say, but also because of the way they limit the thought and speech of group members. Members who violate the taboo on what can be said and thought face the prospect of being cast as traitors and of having their expressions condemned as acts of betrayal. On the matter of betrayal, we may consider a case reported by Connor Friedersdorf in *The Atlantic* (2016).

The case involves a high school student in Minneapolis, Minnesota, who had been active in the "social justice scene." In working for social justice, this student believed he was doing something "noble." He was not, however, wholly in agreement with the views of the groups working for social justice. He was concerned about what he referred to as "pro-censorship tendencies, fixation with intersectionality, and constant uproar over seemingly trivial and innocuous matters like 'cultural appropriation' and 'microaggressions'" and found these preoccupations inconsistent with his "civil-libertarian sensibilities."

According to Friedersdorf, "interacting with social-justice groups made up of high school and college students, he increasingly found himself having to bite his tongue." In the student's words: "I never voiced my personal disagreements because having dissenting views is strictly forbidden in the activist circles I was a part of." If you are not person of color, you will be treated as a "bad ally." If you are a person of color, what you say will be dismissed as a form of "internalized racism," "internalized sexism," or "respectability politics." As a result of comments he made about trigger warnings, he was accused of insensitivity and held responsible for causing members of his cohort to have "traumatic breakdowns." When he criticized campus activists who disrupted controversial speakers, he was accused of being a "respectable negro," an "uncle tom," and a "local coon."

Those who are, like this student, by origin members of a group, but who do not speak as members are meant to speak, have been aptly referred to as "special kinds of traitors" (Friedersdorf, 2016). They are individuals whose race, ethnicity, gender, or other attributes make them part of a group but who fail to adhere to the ideology of that group, most notably its special standing to adjudicate and control speech. For them, there is no more tolerance of freedom of speech than for those who are outside the group; possibly less. And the situation they find themselves in makes it clear that membership in the group is limited not only by race, ethnicity, gender, sexuality, or other identity categories, but by a commitment to controlling speech and thought. That is, it is not shared attributes or even shared experience that makes you a member of the group, but a shared *internal division of thoughts* into the acceptable and the unacceptable. This dividing line constitutes the shared knowledge of self and other held by group members. For those who are, by origin, members of the group, to reject this way of knowing is to undermine a basic pillar of group life.

The community of virtue

In cases such as the one just described, the thoughts divided between acceptable and unacceptable are predominantly thoughts about suffering and loss. They include thoughts about responsibility for suffering and the virtue of suffering, which is to say: the value of suffering and its connection to moral attributes such as innocence and goodness. They are internal struggles over assigning responsibility for suffering to self or other, to those in the group or to those outside. They are thoughts about the meaning and value of the experience of oppression and the goodness and virtue of those who have been oppressed. They are, therefore, thoughts about the link between innocence and victimization.

All of these thoughts have to do with matters of moral judgment and experiences of injustice. In its preoccupation with matters of this kind, the group organized around the end of controlling thoughts establishes itself as a *moral system*. In other words, the group exists to manage matters of good and bad, guilt and innocence, pride and shame. What is essential about the moral orientation to the world is that it blocks thinking to assure that there will always be, in its place, the activity of moral judgment and that such judgment will always favor group members. Judgment that favors group members is judgment that preserves their connection with the good, or, in psychoanalytic language, the "good object." Specifically, in the group organized around a moral purpose, the entire construction of the world and the relationship between interpretation and knowing implied in it are shaped by the work of protecting the good object (in this case represented in the group and its leaders) from the thought that it might not be good.

Loyalty to the group is loyalty of belief in the goodness of the good object. Put simply, the group is the vehicle that protects its members from knowing that the good object is not good, or is not always and altogether good, or that the group member's relationship with the good object also involves a considerable measure of hate: hate directed toward both the group and the self. Thinking means giving up unthought assumptions about the reality of the object and the member's relationship with it. If the goodness of the object is not a given, but something to think about, doubt about that object can be known, spoken, and heard. To control what is known and what can be spoken and heard, then, is psychologically equivalent to protecting all that is good in the world of the group. Accordingly, acts of "betrayal," such as those undertaken by the students described above, take on the meaning of destroying all that is good in the world (of the group), forsaking group members to a world without goodness, "a world ruled by the devil" (Fairbairn, 1952, p. 67).

Just as the distinction between judgment and understanding is at the heart of campus controversy, it is at the heart of how we conceive the mission of the university. Is the mission of the university to guide students and student groups in managing moral judgments of right and wrong, good and bad? Or, is the mission of the university to facilitate students' development of the capacity to move toward an understanding of self and other that is not about good and bad? Does the university sanction and encourage the embedding of students in groups and group identities? Or does the university provide a space where the student may distinguish himself from, or separate himself from, the demands of group life?

We believe these questions, while complex, have clear answers, for, to the extent that the university encourages attachment of students to groups that instantiate a moral purpose, it cannot at the same time sponsor freedom of expression, which always risks betraying the moral standing of the group by calling into question the goodness of its good object. This underlying reality creates the dilemma in which the university finds itself when it attempts to manage the two kinds of freedom implicated in the struggle over free speech. In approaching this dilemma, the university might take more seriously the way these two kinds of freedom (freedom to think and freedom to block thought) map onto corollary notions of safety and safe space.

The first kind of "safety," discussed in the beginning of this chapter, is the feeling attained when the individual is securely embedded in a group or community and has adapted her identity to the identity associated with membership in that group or community, which is a world of those "like us." This kind of space is "safe" because those who are not like us are excluded from it. Doubt about the good, represented by those unlike us, is kept outside. The second kind of "safety" is the safety that by protecting students from assaultive communication seeks to facilitate their ability to carry on a free internal dialogue, in part by moving outside the group, or by exercising forms of autonomy, self-determination, and understanding while within the group. These two notions of safety stand opposed, in that one is the safety that protects us from our thoughts by assuring we will not be called on to think them, while the other is the safety to think our thoughts freely. To move in the direction of the second kind of "safe space" means to weaken the attachment of the student to the group, which very well might include her attachment to the university when conceived as a group (e.g., the "university community").

In the context of free speech, a safe space is a space in which it is possible to think about words and what they mean to self and other, and, in so doing, to diffuse some of their power. It is a space in which it is possible to understand that different ideas can be represented by the same words and that the presence of those with different ideas need not be equated with assault. More important than its potential for managing conflict with others, then, would be the potential use of safe spaces in universities to link words to ideas, and so to provide opportunities to deal internally with the confusion and anger words may provoke. This internal processing of emotion makes it possible to move from forms of conflict rooted in vulnerability, hate, and projection to those organized around thinking, resilience, and mutual regard.

To make the university a safe space for thought and expression, those in positions of responsibility would need to overcome the impulse to treat selected groups of students as objects whose presence makes the university into a "virtuous community." In other words, the university must make a definitive break with the ideal of itself as a *moral system* that can protect those in it from the dangers posed to them by adverse moral judgment. For this to happen, universities and university members would have to give up the hope that they can make themselves "good" by aligning themselves with, identifying with, or colluding with objects (students and identity groups) that are made "good" by an innocence born of real and fantasized victimization.

This divestment of hope would require that faculty and administrators overcome the impulse to divide students along the lines of their own divided selves: Good and bad, innocent and guilty, victim and victimizer. Psychologically, the division of students along the lines of race, gender, ethnicity, and sexual orientation has been used precisely to this effect: as an externalization of morally charged internal divisions. We have argued, and will continue to argue in the following chapter, that doing so has, in many cases, entrenched and intensified those divisions both in the inner worlds of participants and in the world of the university. Using students as players in a moral drama exacerbates the difficulties students face in separating themselves from the demands made on them by identity groups and the insistence, on the part of those groups, that groups take on a central role in managing the challenges associated with identity.

CHAPTER FOUR

Collusion in the university

University campuses are not merely backdrops against which identity-based conflicts play out. Rather, universities are participants, interlocutors, adversaries, or allies—or, in some instances, complex combinations of all of these—in such conflicts. In recent years, universities in the United States, the United Kingdom, Western Europe, and elsewhere have faced what *The Economist* (2012) summarizes as a "tornado of change." Or, to borrow Staley's and Trinkle's geological metaphor: "The landscape of higher education ... is changing rapidly and disruptively ... [is] metaphorically crossed with fault lines ... and is as 'seismic' as it has been in decades" (2011). The disruptions referred to here are associated with economic globalization, competition in the higher education market, information technologies, changing student demographics, contested roles for tenured and non-tenured faculty, tuition costs and educational lending, and public and private sources of university funding. Each of these has been cited as a cause of upheaval in the academic realm (see e.g., Blackmore & Kandinko, 2012; Gornitzka, 1999; Sagaria, 2007).

The conflicts with which we are concerned in this book are occurring in the context of widespread uncertainty about the place and role of the university. Most universities are already contending with considerable pressures, arising both from within and without, to revise their operations, their "missions," and their conceptions of themselves. Campus conflicts that involve the university as a primary actor, therefore, tend to highlight a question with which universities are already struggling: the question of the university's basic nature and purpose.

This question can be formulated in the language of organizational identity. Organizational identity may be understood in terms of organization members' shared beliefs about "who [they] are as an organization," and, therefore, about what is "central, enduring, and distinctive" about their organization's activities, boundaries, and character (Diamond, 2017; Whetten, 2006, p. 220). Although the dynamics of identity development and identity maintenance at the individual level are not the same as those at the organizational level, in both cases the project of defining and sustaining an identity involves the question of the value invested in core qualities, characteristics, and purposes.

The struggle to achieve and maintain identity may be considered among the organization's most important tasks. In establishing its identity, an organization, like an individual, looks both within and outside. This is because, as we have discussed, identity is both the way we know ourselves and the way others know us, and because the way we know ourselves is involved with the way we are known by others. Like an individual, an organization must manage the boundary between inside and outside, a boundary that establishes its separate identity, while also connecting it to the world outside. Managing this boundary involves attending to and protecting what is "inside," engaging meaningfully with what is "outside," and forming links between inside and outside that strengthen, rather than weaken, the boundary.

For both organizations and individuals, managing the boundary between inside and outside requires setting limits in order to focus on tasks germane to principal goals. The failure to establish such limits leads to situations in which activities that serve emotional ends—doing the work that defends against anxiety, or doing the work of propagating fantasies about the organization—come to be prioritized over tasks associated with the organization's "real" work, even undermining the ability of the organization to know what its "real" work is.

The failure to define and affirm boundaries is a critical element of organizational failure, since it assures that the real work of the organization will be poorly done by blurring the distinction between that work and imposed, irrelevant, and even counterproductive activities. In this chapter, we argue that in universities there is a substantial degree of collusion between faculty, students, and external constituencies, expressed in a shared effort to undermine work directed toward universities' primary task, which we identify as teaching and learning. This collusion erodes boundaries established to protect that task. Ironically, this erosion of boundaries is motivated by perceived needs to redeem aspects of universities' organizational identities; that is, to assure that the work undertaken in universities "matters." We contend that university organizations, having lost sight of their primary obligations, now both collude with and exploit those who work and study in them.

There are several types of organizational boundary erosion that may be observed when examining contemporary universities. The first involves a change in the nature and degree of interpenetration between universities and the communities and societies in which they are located. After we examine this change and its meaning for university organizations, we turn to a related, but somewhat less frequently examined, boundary erosion: the erosion of the boundary between the university and the family or home. Alongside efforts to tear down the "Ivory Tower" and demolish the "campus walls" thought to inhibit students from meaningful engagement with the world, there has been a countervailing (and possibility reactionary) movement whereby universities conceive themselves, or wish to conceive themselves, as home-like settings, places that offer comfort, belonging, and safety that are, ultimately, damaging to the university as an organization and to the work meant to go on there.

The university enmeshed with the community

Amid debates about the place of the university, some commentators have suggested that the university is no longer a relevant or productive institution for our time (see McGettigan, 2013; Schrecker, 2010). While many disagree with this assessment, even dissenters tend to frame their objections in instrumental terms. That is, *if* universities matter, their importance is measured by their productivity, especially their capacity to train students for their vocations, or, their (frequently economic) contributions to the "communities" of which they are regarded as members.

The term "community," in higher education discourses, has come to mean many things: It seems to apply not only to the neighborhoods surrounding university campuses, but to regional, national, or international "communities," to the "intellectual community," to various identity-based "communities," and more. In most cases, for the university to fare well in its internal and external self-assessments, it must offer demonstrations of its contribution to some or all these communities, a contribution typically referred to as its "social impact." What remains consistent within this debate, then, is the premise that the boundary between the university and the world outside must be broken down, that it is an impediment to, rather than a necessary basis for, teaching and learning.

We should emphasize that the defense of a meaningful boundary between university and external constituencies and interests does not imply the absence of significant interaction across that boundary. Most notably, it does not diminish the importance of the work of the university in preparing students for employment and for participation in civic life. As with the self-boundary that protects the individual's inner world and secures access to the individual's internal source of initiative and creative thought, the boundary that separates the university from the world outside assures the possibility that the work done in the university will not be all about adaptation to external pressures, but that it will, at least to a significant degree, express an internal source of initiative, creative thinking, and self-determination in shaping identity.

Perhaps surprisingly, there are relatively few voices advocating the separation to which we have just referred (see Bowker, 2012). There are few educational leaders who defend the idea that the capacity of the contemporary university to "matter" may actually depend on its ability to establish a space devoted to teaching and learning that is buffered from "communities" and their pressures, which include the demands of labor markets, trends in local and national politics, norms of mass culture, criteria for belonging to groups, and the like. As Robert Nisbet argues, there was once "a kind of social contract" between universities and such "outside" agents and forces according to which universities agreed to limit their direct involvement in political, social, cultural, and economic affairs if, in exchange, this self-limitation permitted university members to perform the work of teaching and learning without excessive intrusion (1971, p. 199). This "social contract" is in many respects antithetical to the collusion we treat in this chapter, since this contract implies an important separation between universities and outside forces that distract the university from its real work.

To say as much is not to idealize a type of university that is unconcerned with the world outside. Rather, it is to note a difference in ways of conceiving the purpose of the university: one in which the instrumentality of the university's relationship to the outside world leads to an adaptive and compliant orientation within the university with respect to its work; the other in which the maintenance of a boundary between the university and the outside world offers students and faculty a degree of freedom to engage their work in more creative, more autonomous, and less adaptive and compliant ways. Put another way, we might imagine the value of the university to be found not in its ability to offer specific goods or services directly to this or that particular community but, rather, in its establishment of a space where individuals can learn and grow. It is, of course, a subtle matter, one of degree and emphasis, but we may say that, in one vision of the university, the services offered are really *for* students, rather than for students' (present and future) services *to* outside entities.

Indeed, until fairly recently, "the service rendered by the university [was considered to] lay not so much in what it did, but in what it was … a unique environment for young minds [and] their disciplined exposure to scholarship" (Nisbet, 1971, p. 34). If, for a moment, the university could be imagined as an individual, then we might say that the university once enjoyed a greater degree of "ontological security" than it does today: a certain confidence in itself, a clarity about what it was, a sense of value in being what it was, and an (internal) mandate to do the work that proceeded from its being. Here, the university's capacity to resist calls to adapt to or comply with various external pressures would be essential to fulfilling its identity and its purpose.

Over the past half-century, however, universities have embraced a vision of themselves as direct service providers and "change agents" in their communities. Universities have gradually redefined themselves as sites of scientific and technological innovation, leaders in efforts to intervene in matters of pressing socio-political concern, centers for vocational training and rehabilitation, micro-engines of employment, entrepreneurship, and economic growth, and "partners" with corporate and governmental entities.

Most universities today emphasize rather than minimize their interdependence with the communities that house them. This emphasis may be seen not only in the rapidly expanding number of community-based learning and service-based learning programs that strive to integrate higher learning with the communities that lie "beyond the campus walls" (see e.g., Courtney, 2009; Curtis, 2001; Kolb & Kolb, 2009), but in reorientations of university curricula toward the delivery of "marketable" degrees and transferrable skills to students who will emerge from the university with "real world" experience in high growth fields.

While teaching and learning that prepares students for their lives when they graduate is certainly consistent with the purpose of the university, the more instrumentally the university's role is conceived, the more the university tends to forget that what makes an employee, a member of a civic association, or even a member of the broader civil society valuable is her capacity to think, create, and act. Although they need not be, these capacities tend to be neglected the more universities merge their ends with those of corporations, public institutions, or non-profit organizations. When the education of students is conceived as a sociopolitical project in which the student's education is an instrument for or means of satisfying the ends of employers, communities, markets, or nation states, there is little room for the kind of teaching and learning that facilitates creativity and self-determination.

The university as family and home

At the same time that universities have sought to cast themselves as centers of change, technological and economic engines, and players on the global political stage, they have also blurred the line distinguishing them from home and family. Many universities describe themselves as a "family of learners" and a "home away from home." In addition to explicit suggestions that they be understood as families or homes, universities offer a bevy of services and amenities to students that have something of a domestic quality, including, but not limited to: twenty-four-hour technical support hotlines, four-year "graduation guarantees," "personalized" teams of tutors, academic coaches, financial planners, career advisers, state-of-the-art dining, athletic, health, recreation, entertainment, and computing facilities, and various programs and personnel devoted to enhancing students' well-being, "engagement," and "campus life."

Today's student is encouraged to believe that most, if not all, needs and desires, even those having nothing to do with higher education, can be met in connection with the university, just as the child is encouraged to believe, at least at first and with a great deal of accuracy, that most if not all needs may be met in connection with the family. Part of this effort is inextricable from the premise that the university is a place where the student's personal wellness will be attended to, not only incidentally, but as a top priority.

As a part of this effort, universities have placed great emphasis on the collaborative and communal aspects of learning, to a point where the individual student may, as Michael Godsey (2015) has suggested, feel "engulfed" by regular urgings toward togetherness and close-knit interaction. Community-based learning programs, academic learning communities, interactive group projects, and collaborative learning environments emphasize togetherness in a way that is also reminiscent of family and home, where cohesion may become a priority overriding individual family members' needs for separateness, difference, and solitary activity.

If the university not only calls itself a home and family but behaves in ways that emulate aspects of home life, we should not be surprised if university members expect that obligations associated with the family be fulfilled by the university. In assuming home-like qualities, the university colludes with students' efforts to continue or reinitiate roles as members of a family. And while we may be tempted to see only the contradictions between the marketization of the university, on one hand, and its provision of a nurturing "home" for students on the other, these departures from the work of teaching and learning ultimately support each other. For instance, the establishment of a community-oriented center devoted to the meeting of social problems may not only bring in revenue from outside sources, but may provide assurances to university members that the university shares their moral orientation to the world and that their beliefs will be affirmed by the university, as they might be in a family. At the same time, the offering of luxurious amenities to students cannot be separated from institutional financial motivations, such as the recruitment and retention of students.

Given the multiple intrusions into university organizations and their work, we may not be wrong to imagine the contemporary university as "multiphrenic," to borrow a term from Kenneth Gergen, since it wishes to retain "the accumulated luster of the university" associated with its traditional teaching and learning activities (Nisbet, 1971, p. 195), while also advertising itself as a pillar of the community, an economic engine, a center of political activism, a therapeutic community, a place of socialization, an entertainment facility, and a second home for students. And since it has been the "accumulated" prestige of the university that, paradoxically, has given it license to diverge from the very tasks that once gave it prestige, we may ask why so many (students, faculty, and administrators) would continue to be drawn to universities in their current form, in spite of rising tuition costs, declines in the value of university degrees, evidence of a general fall-off in academic rigor, and questionable levels of enmeshment with forces and constituencies in the community and the broader society.

Universities have shown considerable willingness to accede to demands of various protesters and protest groups, to collude with unrealistic beliefs about university members' roles and powers, and even to accept responsibility for injustices occurring on (and off) their campuses. In some cases, universities' acts of contrition and admissions of guilt have affirmed their roles as victimizers of students. Given their interests in maintaining positive reputations, we may wonder why universities would be willing to concede as much and why university members would continue to belong to university organizations if they are confessedly guilty. Part of the answer is that even if universities themselves must take on the role of victimizers, a crucial premise underlying a sought-after collusion between universities and students is confirmed: that the real enemies in the battle for identity, meaning, and "mattering" are external, which is to say that the objects of students' anger are to be found in the external (and not inner, psychic) world, and that they may be meaningfully engaged in the context of university life. Whether acting as protectors of victims or confessing their own failures, universities take up positions in the struggle against various sorts of victimization to assure themselves sustainable roles in dramas that seem to "matter" a great deal to university members and community members alike.

Universities collude with students and take on roles in dramas of victimization when they explicitly or implicitly agree that they are a source (or the source) of students' anxieties and an appropriate target (or the most appropriate target) for students' protest and rage. While universities may, of course, contribute to identity-based tensions, they may take on responsibilities for feelings of oppression and victimization that originate elsewhere. In doing so, they affirm the paradigm or explanatory system employed by students who understand the sources of their anxiety as, essentially, external.

Of course, all organizations must validate the beliefs, experiences, and fantasies of their members to some extent, but universities have recently found themselves validating experiences, beliefs, and fantasies inconsistent with their basic principles and values. Perhaps fearful that invalidating university members' (or community members') beliefs, experiences, or fantasies would lead to chaos or organizational dissolution, universities have permitted themselves to take on the role of a "broken home" for those university members who require it.

Put another way, universities are engaged in a special relationship with students who belong to groups understood to be victims of past discrimination and oppression. At the heart of this relationship is a promise that cannot be kept, in other words: that greater opportunity and access to higher education will dispel the disadvantages faced by members of such groups, both in educational institutions and in the broader society. Collusion plays an important role in this relationship, because the promise expresses a tacit agreement that, since the disadvantages facing these groups can be understood as the result of historical injustices, all parties can ignore the reality that something *more* than rectifying injustice is needed to overcome those disadvantages.

That is, rectifying injustice cannot overcome the problems that arise due to identification with a degraded group self. On the contrary, the more emphasis is placed on the group identities of students, and on the idea that a degraded identity can be overcome by forcing a shift in the valences of group identities from negative to positive, the more students find themselves in a double bind. At the same time, the celebration of oppression that ties students to such groups has become integral to the identities of university members who do not belong to them (particularly to (white) faculty and administrators). These individuals can no more give up their attachment to playing roles in dramas of oppression and victimization than can members of oppressed and victimized groups. As a consequence, university administrations fail to set boundaries that would make it clear that acquiescing to demands of identity-based groups reinforces a fantasy antithetical to the ends of higher education, including the end of facilitating the development of a secure and resilient identity.

Initiatives arising out of social movements of the last half of the twentieth century such as affirmative action, when applied to universities, could reasonably be argued to right a serious wrong, which is the prevention of women, minority students, and others from access to higher education. It is not that the ideal driving such movements is unimportant, nor that the specific initiatives set forth are ineffective. Rather, the problem is the conviction that efforts to institute justice (however successful or unsuccessful they may be) will be sufficient to solve the problems caused by injustice. This conviction entails a rejection (or denial) of the idea that there is damage done by injustice that justice cannot fix. The rejection of this idea is an essential element in what we have referred to as the fantasy of the oppressed. This fantasy—shared by members of oppressed groups as well as university leaders—seeks to make universities settings in which the harms caused by past injustices can be confronted and overcome. When such fantasies are operative, universities acquiesce to demands to accept culpability for hidden racism, while attempting to provide students with environments free of the dangers posed by understanding, empathy, and acknowledgement of the complex and enduring wounds of the past.

In other words, several sorts of collusive relationships undertaken by universities involve identification with students as victims. This identification with students' victimized selves—whether the victimization is real, fantasized, or both—naturally suggests that an important part of the university's work is to provide a safe space, family, or home, where victimized students can find belonging, healing, and nurture. But the home-like protective functions the university assumes in this respect do not protect students in the way they need to be protected. To be a home or a family for students-as-victims means protecting students' fantasies of innocence and students' identities as determined by groups of victims and victimizers, rather than protecting organizational and interpersonal boundaries that would permit students safely to explore, challenge, or question these and other aspects of themselves and others. Universities' home-like offerings impede contact with students' real selves and authentic identities, which, for reasons discussed throughout this book, are presumed to be bad and shameful. And, perhaps even more importantly, these collusive efforts are internally inconsistent inasmuch as the homes that universities provide *must fail* to provide appropriate forms of care (i.e., must "break") if the drama of victimization, abandonment, and recrimination is to carry itself out.

The broken home and the absence of empathy

A number of universities have assumed responsibility for important events and prevailing attitudes in their environments in order to offer one form of protection to students: protection from conflict and anxiety associated with difference. If the university apologizes and accepts culpability for not creating an adequately safe and regulated environment, or for not sufficiently adapting to the demands of students, we may say that the university is colluding with expectations that it provide boundaries that protect students from the non-adaptive environments of the world outside, much as the family home once did (or should have done). At the same time, these expectations are inevitably poorly met or not met at all, with the result that students are permitted or, perhaps, invited, to replay in university settings dramas involving parental failure.

Let us consider, on this point, the confusion between the university and the family home in the now well-known exchanges between Yale undergraduate students and faculty members Erika and Nicholas Christakis. Erika Christakis was a lecturer in early childhood education and a faculty member in residence at Yale's Silliman House; Nicholas Christakis a professor of sociology and medicine and a faculty member in residence, also at Silliman. In October of 2015, Erika Christakis ignited a debate about free speech, psychological safety, and the respective duties of students, faculty, and the university when she replied to concerns about students wearing culturally insensitive Halloween costumes by sending an email message, which argued, in part:

> Today we seem afraid that college students are unable to decide how to dress themselves on Halloween … I wonder if we should reflect more transparently, as a community, on the consequences of an institutional (bureaucratic and administrative) exercise of implied control over college students … Have we lost faith in young people's capacity—in your capacity—to exercise self-censure, through social norming, and also in your capacity to ignore or reject things that trouble you? (quoted in Friedersdorf, 2015)

While Christakis' message was in many ways an illuminating reflection on campus politics, Christakis would soon discover she was mistaken in presuming that control and censorship in universities arise primarily from bureaucrats and administrators, rather than from students. In response to her email, students protested, demanded punitive measures, and composed an open letter accusing her of "degrad[ing] marginalized people" and of "infantiliz[ing] the student body" (Friedersdorf, 2015). This latter accusation is particularly striking, since, on the contrary,

Christakis' message was a critique of infantilization in that she urged students to contend with difference and to negotiate conflict as adults, in a civil manner, and in a diverse educational environment, without calling on the university to exercise the regulatory (and paternalistic) function of settling disagreements for them.

After the incident, Nicholas Christakis offered to communicate about the issue with various groups of students. In one exchange captured on video, a group of students shouted at him, while others departed, saying: "He doesn't deserve to be listened to." Nicholas stated explicitly what Erika had advocated implicitly in her remarks: that the job of a faculty member at a university is to provide an intellectually rich—although not necessarily conflict-free—environment in which students can learn. During these remarks, one student screamed at him to "be quiet" and insisted that he had "failed" to perform his job, which was to provide "a place of comfort and home" for students. She demanded that Nicholas resign his position because he was unwilling or unable to understand that his job was "not about creating an intellectual space," but, rather, about creating "a home here" (Drezner, 2015). In another recorded exchange, students wept and accused Nicholas of "gaslighting" them when he refused to admit that his words were "an expression of racism" and "an act of violence." While he apologized (and later resigned) for having "caused [students] pain" (Kirchik, 2016), this apology and acceptance of culpability was inadequate for the students, who felt most aggrieved by his and his wife's words.

An important aspect of the conflict was exposed when students displayed particularly intense emotions at Nicholas' suggestion that, even though he may differ from students in race, gender, and other attributes, they *could* understand something of each other through open dialogue. When the students rejected this claim, Nicholas asked: "Then what is the reason that you ask to be heard, by me or anyone else?" At this moment, one student approached him closely, saying: "You and I are not the same person … Your experiences will never connect to mine. Empathy is not necessary for you to understand that you are wrong" (Kirchik, 2016).

Amidst claims from the crowd that "this is our home" and that our "home is broken," another student addressed Nicholas directly, saying: "This is my home and you came in here. You adapt to me. Do you understand that? You take care of me. And you haven't been doing that. And I've kept quiet" (Kirchik, 2016). These students seemed particularly interested in, even preoccupied with, obtaining an apology from the Christakises, not only for causing them pain but for something much deeper. They seemed to wish Nicholas, in particular, to acknowledge a major moral failing that involved a willful abandonment of students. Indeed, what students seemed to want was for Nicholas willingly to assume the role of the bad object. Since, according to one student, "empathy is not necessary" for Nicholas to take on this role, students became confused and frustrated by his apparent resistance to doing so.

As Nicholas continued to demonstrate that he was interested in engaging in conversation and in understanding what was being asked of him, the students became increasingly frustrated and even enraged. It is difficult, in watching these videos, not to see what Nicholas might have seen more quickly: that students were not interested in conversation and understanding but in an unqualified apology. "We just want an acknowledgement of hurt and we have yet to get that," one student explained. "So, are you going to say that or not? Because I can just leave if you're not going to say that." Frustrated with Nicholas' hesitation, the student broke down emotionally and expressed confusion about what was "holding [him] back," asking, rhetorically: "Do you need to know what you're apologizing for?"

What students were demanding, then, was an unreserved apology for the Christakises' failings and, later, expulsions from their positions, primarily because they were insufficiently aligned with the experiences, beliefs, and fantasies of the groups of students most directly impacted by this event. To some extent, Nicholas colluded with students in his response when he stated that he felt surprised that students "weren't able to form an opinion of me as a human being and what my beliefs are, and to see the extent to which they are in agreement with your beliefs. You seem to think that somehow I don't agree with the content of your beliefs." In this case, rather than addressing the meaning of being on "different sides," Nicholas attempted to convince students that he was on "their" side, that he was "like them," that he was in their group and shared their beliefs.

The students, ultimately, rejected all of these arguments and insisted that both Nicholas and Erika Christakis resign. In response, both resigned from their positions at Silliman, and Erika resigned from her faculty position at Yale. Although Nicholas remains a faculty member, his comments after the incident suggest that he may have internalized the accusations of his students, even accepting culpability for the affair. "I care so much about the same issues you [students] care about," he said. "I have the same beliefs that you do … I'm genuinely sorry, and to have disappointed you. I've disappointed myself" (Stanley-Becker, 2015).

The resignations of the Christakises, along with Nicholas' apology and admission of disappointment and failure, reflect a form of collusion between university faculty, university leaders, and students who effectively (re)defined the function of the university in light of this dispute. Soon after the incident, a Yale student wrote an essay—since removed—for the Yale *Herald* laying out the case that the Christakises' jobs were not to create an "intellectual space," but "to make Silliman a safe space that all students can come home to … where your experiences are a valid concern to the administration and where you can feel free to talk with them about your pain without worrying that the conversation will turn into an argument every single time." The article continued: "He [Nicholas Christakis] doesn't get it. And I don't want to debate. I want to talk about my pain" (quoted in Goldberg, 2015).

In this incident, we can see how the confusion between university and home is reinforced, such that students respond to putative failures of faculty to meet expectations derived from the premise that a university must be like a family home, where members share a set of core experiences and beliefs, and where certain thoughts and expressions are forbidden. What is more, the specific nature of the family- and home-environment demanded by students is one in which inappropriate forms of care and protection are offered. Although the student's essay cited above suggests that a home ought to be a place where "your experiences are a valid concern" and "where you can feel free" to "talk about [your] pain," the real emphasis in the essay is on a kind of safety, safety from "argument," "debate," and conflict, and, therefore, safety from challenges to beliefs, fantasies, or defenses, particularly those involving experiences of victimization. But argument, debate, challenge, and confrontation with difference are essential ingredients in the forms of relating called for in civil life—that is, life outside the family group—for which the university putatively prepares students.

If the university is to be a place that privileges safety from difference and enforces other norms commonly associated with families, then it is to be a kind of extended (and likely unsatisfying) home, where university members engage each other with compassion, but not with empathy: two concepts we have distinguished in this book, particularly in Chapter One. Compassion means relating by way of identification, and entails the confirmation of beliefs, experiences, fantasies, or defenses. The demands cited above, that a professor offer apologies that need not be understood, not attempt to empathize but simply accept that he is wrong, and not engage in "argument" or "debate," but, rather, comply with students' demands and affirm their attributions, all may be understood as demands that experiences of "pain" in interactions with fellow university members be treated with a form of relating that overrides rational thought and discussion.

The form of compassion demanded by Yale students means that students' communications of their experiences must not be questioned, analyzed, or doubted. It is particularly important *not* to have one's communications questioned, analyzed, or doubted if these communications must be immediately validated by others in order to maintain an identity that prevents contact with a self imagined to be bad or shameful. Compassion, then, becomes synonymous with protection, not from impingement or exploitation but from contact with what is real and active in the self. Of course, what is real and active in the self is precisely what is feared to be bad or shameful.

In earlier chapters, we have explored at some length the challenges involved in having one's fantasies of victimization and oppression (fantasies, for instance, about others' intent to do harm) exposed or understood. One of the ways such fantasies might be illuminated is through empathic exchanges in which the true nature of the wishes, beliefs, and experiences that have shaped them are examined in a benign and non-judgmental environment. But if the students involved in the incident at Yale are right, then, on the contrary, universities are places where an *absence* of empathy is the foundation of students' safety. A student is only "safe," in this case, if he knows that his experience and his fantasies are protected from being known by others, and in feeling certain, for instance, that he may lodge a complaint and demand an apology without engaging in the work of communication or understanding. Empathic relationships between university members, on the other hand, would be relationships in which university members would be permitted, and even encouraged, to communicate about and understand the nature of the experiences, relationships, and beliefs in question, and, in turn, to communicate about and understand the real dilemmas expressed by all parties.

There is no reason to suspect that the feelings expressed by campus protesters in recent years—feelings of danger, threat, victimization, and marginalization—are "unreal," and yet the fantasy dimension in them cannot be ignored. Part of the importance of being "in pain," as we have discussed in earlier chapters, is that being in pain implies a role in a drama of victimization: a role that, in turn, implies innocence. To be a victim, or to adopt the identity of a victim, is to safeguard one's innocence against suspicions about the value of the self. The unconscious (shared, collusive) conviction that the child's self is worthless intensifies the need to belong to a "good" family and/or an innocent group, just as it drives the projective mechanisms through which "bad" qualities are placed outside in those who differ. The insistence that others who differ are responsible for the suffering associated with our identification with a bad self also implies the loss of internal control, action, and initiative, making others bear responsibility for the harm we do to ourselves and to others.

Of course, if, in the end, these efforts do not leave students feeling truly "safe," perhaps we should not be too surprised. Without empathy and understanding, how can voicing a complaint be a meaningful act? How can the receipt of an apology be comforting if the apologizer does not have to understand that for which he apologizes? The precariousness of social defense systems employed by groups and universities is on display here, as words and deeds are divorced from meaningful content but are, nevertheless, policed and controlled with vigilance in attempts to replay and, perhaps, master roles in dramas involving abandonment and victimization.

Indeed, since fantasies of victimization are deeply ambivalent, danger is *required* in order to feel secure in the belief that one is endangered. Thus, fantasies of victimization must, paradoxically, be kept "safe" by university members, who must behave in ways that confirm the reality of student's imperilment. University members, therefore, must agree that students are harmed, or must agree to harm or to have harmed students, in order to validate fantasies of victimization. This collusive agreement may be understood as an effort to keep students "safe" from a very different sort of harm.

Intrusion and expulsion

So far, we have considered the university's enmeshment with the larger community, serving the community by erasing boundaries between the university and the world outside, and deriving its importance from the more or less direct contributions it makes to the community. We have also considered the university's problematic attempt to act as a surrogate family home for students. To the extent that the university conceives of itself as a community member, it exploits university members to perform work that is not truly germane to the organization's purpose. And to the extent that the university conceives of itself as a family home, it protects students *not* from undue influence and pressure, but from opportunities to engage in reflection and dialogue that may hold educational value. When combined, these two types of boundary erosion risk transforming universities into broken homes and exploitative families, organizations that provide problematic forms of care and protection while simultaneously (ab)using students to shore up universities' senses of identity and importance.

One of the most common ways organizations contend with negative experiences—which may include anything from frustration and disappointment to operational failure or scandal—is to validate them while simultaneously distancing them from the organization. If it is possible to find an external source of blame on which to project inadequate, offensive, or other "bad" attributes, then the organization has found a simple remedy. But, even when this solution is available, there is also pressure to identify individuals or groups within the organization as guilty parties. If the university identifies guilty parties, then corrections, punishments, or (literal or figurative) expulsions may be enacted to externalize the bad, and to preserve the identity and legitimacy of the organization.

Consider, for instance, the response by officials at the University of Oklahoma to a widely circulated cellphone video of a group of Sigma Alpha Epsilon (SAE) fraternity members singing a racist chant on a chartered bus. When the video went public, the university quickly expelled two students, and disciplined more than two dozen others, while the SAE fraternity house on campus was closed, its doors literally shuttered and its windows boarded (Svrluga, 2015). The university and the national SAE organization seemed to do their best to distance the offending individuals from their organizations. The students involved—who were not the first students to use racial slurs at a small, private gathering, and who, as it turns out, learned the chant at a national SAE leadership event (Svrluga, 2015)—became scapegoats, literally removed from the university campus in the hope that doing so would be sufficient to affirm the identity of the university as good, nonracist, and identified with concerns for racial and social justice.

In his public communications, University President David Boren repeatedly used the term, "snuff out," when discussing his course of action: "There seems to be a culture [of racism] in some of these fraternities," he said, "and it just has to be snuffed out." "If we're ever going to snuff this out in the whole country," he continued, "we're going to have to have zero tolerance" (McLoughlin, 2015). "Snuff out" is a powerful phrase, meaning to violently suffocate. Boren's use of it should remind us that angry and violent reactions may be provoked not only when we witness an offense, but when we fear that we may identify ourselves (or "know" ourselves) in connection with the offense. When extreme and unforgiving (e.g., "zero-tolerance") punishments are applied to those who offend us, we violently "expel" them in the hope that doing so will reassure us about "who we are," which is really "who we must be" in the eyes of others.

For Boren, once a person has committed an offense of this kind, he apparently forfeits membership in the university organization. Boren's official response to the incident informed "those who have misused their free speech in such a reprehensible way … you have violated all that we stand for. You should not have the privilege of calling yourselves [Oklahoma] 'Sooners'" (Worland, 2015). With these (odd) words, Boren expelled the students from the university "family" and "snuffed out," as it were, their identities as Sooners, just as the national SAE organization literally locked offending students out of their campus home.

This coordinated response reflects an effort to protect the university and fraternity organizations from any association with racism. It colludes with students' fantasies of identity-based danger and victimization via the mechanism of scapegoating, which singles out a small number of intolerably "bad" individuals and suggests that the struggle to safeguard meaningful identities is waged by expelling them from the university group, even so far as to take away their (group, family) identity (i.e., "the privilege of calling [themselves] Sooners"). That is, the university colludes with the premise that racist attitudes arising from outside the group are the primary threats to students, confirming the fantasy that students would be safe if only such outsiders could be eliminated; or, to put it a bit differently, if, by expelling certain individuals, the university and its members could convince themselves that the real dangers have been *always already* outside. By colluding with students' externalization of what is bad or damaging in their identity-based struggles, universities help students feel vindicated in a battle against injustice. But, in doing so, universities weaken, rather than strengthen, students' capacities to acknowledge and confront the forces in their inner worlds that cause them to feel such intense anxiety, rage, and shame when encountering racist attitudes and actions.

Racist attitudes are unlikely to be eliminated from the university (or any other) organization. Denying this fact by attempting to purge the university of offending elements is not only doomed to fail to prevent racism on campus in the future, but suggests that the goal of protests on university campuses may not be to eliminate racism but, rather, to engage in perpetual conflict about racism, to facilitate ongoing conflict, and to permit repeated expulsions of offenders from the group: processes that ultimately expresses the ambivalent conviction that in spite of our best efforts, what is bad and dangerous *will always rise again* within us, and within our beloved groups and families.

On this point, we must consider the stunning organizational responses to discoveries of sexist, racist, and otherwise offensive private communications by student-athletes at Harvard University, Columbia University, Princeton University, Washington University, and Amherst College. Each of these universities recently suspended or disciplined members of athletic teams for messages exchanged by small numbers of individuals. While members of these universities were understandably troubled and hurt by the publication of these conversations, the individuals engaged in those conversations were not responsible for their publication and did not distribute them to the persons or groups derogated therein. That is, the messages, in themselves, were not intended to harass, threaten, or harm others. Although there is a persuasive argument to be made that private communications by students are of no concern to universities, the most common reaction to the universities' responses has been protest and outrage that the punishments of these students were not harsh enough.

The justification offered for disciplining students for engaging in lewd, racist, sexist, or hateful private speech has been virtually identical across the five aforementioned universities. Columbia University released two statements in late 2016 in which it argued: "Columbia University has zero tolerance in its athletics programs for the group messaging and texts sent by several members of the men's varsity wrestling team. They are appalling, at odds with the core values of the University, violate team guidelines, and have no place in our community" (Martin & Grubic, 2016). In a later statement, the University (disingenuously) claimed to "recognize that free speech is a core value both of the University community and of our nation," and that "our students and faculty have the right to express themselves and their views, whether through their public or private communications. However, the group text messages that have been brought to light do not meet the standard of behavior we expect from our student-athletes at Columbia" (CU Athletics, 2016). At Princeton, Athletic Director Mollie Samann wrote: "We make clear to all of our student-athletes that they represent Princeton University at all times, on and off the playing surface and in and out of season, and we expect appropriate, respectful conduct from them at all times" (Cooney, 2016).

What is troubling here is that, no matter how offensive we may find their words, sanctions against students for using them have been justified using a logic that is virtually indistinguishable from the Orwellian notion of thought-crime. While we might argue about the degree to which incendiary language may be regulated on university campuses, in this case, the messages were private, and therefore equivalent to speaking privately with a confidante, or even thinking or speaking to oneself. The notion that students' speech and conduct may be monitored and evaluated "at all times" and that students are not private persons but representatives of the university both "on and off the playing surface and in and out of season" implies that there is no time or place in which a student's thoughts and expressions may be his own.

In this case, as in others discussed earlier, we find that one kind of "safe space" has displaced another, such that students who were offended by the content of these messages—students who might have directed their anger at the person or persons who made the messages public, rather than at their authors—asserted their right to a space free from contact with insulting and derogatory statements. But the assertion of this kind of safe space means the destruction of a more important kind of safe space: the private space in which it is safe to think or speak whatever thoughts or words come to mind, even if those thoughts or words are, by their nature, insulting, derogatory, vulgar, or offensive.

These universities' efforts to thought-police students by asserting that no communications are private and, therefore, that no students enjoy a private space in which they may express themselves while affiliated with the university, are important parts of a broader attempt to transform the university from a place that facilitates independent thought and autonomous activity into a family-like group that has "zero tolerance" for deviation from its norms. Indeed, these efforts mirror destructive family dynamics in which the thoughts, attitudes, and expressions of children are surveilled and punished to such a degree that children can find no place where it is safe to be. When universities call on students, and particularly on student-athletes, to exercise a higher degree of "self-control," citing their status as representatives of the university, the form of self-control suggested involves not control over conduct and actions affecting others, but control over the inner world in the form of purging (or more accurately repressing) unacceptable thoughts. The idea that the university would establish itself as a place that has the power and authority to repress thoughts, and in this way exert control over the inner world, suggests that the university here represents an external form of a repressive internal authority.

The punishments of these students amount to a demand that students extinguish any aspects of themselves that differ from the values of the university when conceived of as a group or community. Of course, it is grimly ironic that, in many cases, students who participate in lewd, degrading, or insulting communications do so because, on the contrary, these attitudes and expressions are *very much* a part of the (unstated) norms and values (or "culture") of athletic teams, university groups, or the university itself. We might even imagine that when a university punishes a student-athlete for his private thoughts, it is really defending itself against anxiety and shame associated with the discrepancy between the reality of the organization and the norms and values it espouses. Students' private worlds, then, are sacrificed in an attempt to disavow unacceptable knowledge about the university organization itself.

To the extent that punishments or protests directed at university members are efforts to "change the culture" of a university or of a university group, it must also be noted that changing a university's "culture" seems to require regulating the thoughts, attitudes, and expressions of all those who represent it. While the meaning of the term "culture" is contested and complex, we can say that the belief that by applying pressure or punishment to those who violate (stated) values will change or redeem a "culture" reflects at least two fantasies. The first fantasy is that the reality of a university's "culture" is identical to what university leaders or (some) university members wish it to be. That is, there is wishful and magical thinking involved in the belief that a "culture" can be established merely by writing a "mission statement" that "defines" what a university's culture is or should be.

The second fantasy involves the belief that invading the privacy of university members to control errant thoughts and attitudes can redeem a "culture." On the contrary, such invasions are likely to generate rage and hate, the very emotions identified as unacceptable when associated with the language of diversity. Indeed, the university has taken hold of private communication as a way of channeling a significant measure of the aggression found within it, directed that aggression at targets identified as suitable, and enacted a destructive fantasy in the name of purging itself of destructive impulse. Nothing could be less likely to foster mutual tolerance and understanding, especially since purging the "guilty" parties in no way purges (but, rather, serves to legitimize) the destructive impulse directed at them.

On this matter, we should consider the aftermath of the 2015 police shooting of Michael Brown in Ferguson, Missouri, in which student-athletes at the University of Missouri refused to practice or play, while student-led groups staged a number of protests concerning what they described as a "culture of racism" at the university. The specific incidents cited by protesters involved not only the shooting of Brown but reports of individuals—presumably, but not assuredly, students—engaging in racist expressions, including the shouting of a racial slur from a pickup truck and the scrawling of a swastika on a residence hall. These incidents led to accusations levelled at the administration for abetting racism on campus and for "not doing enough to change the culture."

The advocacy group known as "Concerned Student 1950" issued a set of demands to the University. The list included demands that President Tim Wolfe compose a "handwritten apology" to black students, that he hold a press conference in which he "acknowledge his white male privilege," and that he publicly "recognize that systems of oppression exist" (for a compilation of demands from over fifty universities, see: www.thedemands.org). Additional demands included the immediate resignation of Wolfe, mandatory diversity and inclusion training programs, increased funding for centers and services to support students of color, and a commitment to increase the numbers of black faculty and staff to ten percent of university employees by the 2017–2018 academic year.

To the surprise of observers, the university complied with the bulk of these demands. In a public statement given on November 6, 2015, President Wolfe acknowledged that "racism does exist at our university and it is unacceptable. It is a long-standing, systemic problem which daily affects our family of students, faculty and staff." Three days later, Wolfe issued his resignation. Further demands were discussed and efforts continue to be made to meet them, including the (near-impossible) demand that black persons compose ten percent of university faculty and staff in two years (Thompson & Walsh, 2015).

In this case, the university was willing to assume responsibility for the bad acts and attitudes present on (and off) its campus as part of its attempt to expel intolerable elements from its group and to cleanse its "culture." While the outrage of students and protesters is certainly understandable, by acceding not just to the specific demands of protesters but to the premises underlying them, the university colluded with the fantasy that racism can be eradicated by firing a university president, by "training" university members not to be racist, and by hiring or granting tenure to more people of color. In taking these actions, the university failed to give consideration to the possibility that these incidents, and university members' understandable anger triggered by them, did not reflect the university's guilt or its intent to do harm.

What is more, the premise that the appropriate battleground for identity-related conflicts is an external one and that identity-based anxieties are rooted in the university's "culture" suggest that distress about "who we are" can be resolved if others can be monitored, trained, punished, or expelled when they pique our anger. The university's collusive acceptance of responsibility for carrying out this task, then, represents a choice (perhaps an unconscious one) to inculcate a group culture, rather than to define and defend an intellectual space in which internal sources of anger, shame, or confusion related to identity might be safely explored. By taking on this work, the university colludes with students in providing victimizers on demand, confirming rather than challenging students' fantasies and defenses associated with victimization.

Universities' admissions of guilt, terminations of leaders, expulsions of students, and other actions taken in the name of organizational correction, therefore, serve several important functions. Their willingness to collude with the explicit demands and implicit premises of identity-based protests protects the innocence of students by freeing them of culpability for destructive fantasies and actions driven by them. All of this can be considered a part of an effort to protect themselves from their dangerous inner worlds. At the same time, universities would like to hold on to their own sense of innocence: the belief that they are good and that they do good work. Their collusion maintains a social defense system in which almost anything said or done on a university campus "matters," lending importance and gravity (if not also agony) to even seemingly trivial occurrences or events. Collusion also affirms a basic premise that threats to students, to university members, and even to the university as an organization arise from the outside, a premise that may be used to entrench the university's role as a custodian of students (*in loco parentis*) and to cover up internal threats and unrecognized failures, including, most prominently, the failure to protect the boundaries of the university for both faculty and students. In other words, acts of compliance, internalizations of guilt, and expulsions of offending elements operate in a way not entirely unlike screen memories of trauma: They highlight and exaggerate real events while obfuscating deeper, systemic failures and damaged relationships within the organization and its membership.

In spite of the truth of accusations that university campuses are host to a number of serious problems, such as racism and sexual assault, the deepest systemic failure of the university as an organization has been its failure to defend its boundaries. This failure has meant the loss of the unique purpose and identity of the university as a place of teaching and learning, protected not only from labor markets, political powers, and community actors, but from the temptation to transform the space of the university into a space where the work of teaching and learning is displaced by the work of managing group identities, instituting norms appropriate to families and homes, occupying roles in dramas of victimization, and indulging fantasies of protection, guilt, innocence, and recrimination.

The diversity fantasy

Underlying the ideal of diversity is a fantasy, one that may be considered the emotional driver of the university's implementation of diversity-oriented policies and initiatives. These policies and initiatives are typically understood to be an important, if not central, part of the university's mission and are featured prominently in its "vision" of itself in the future. As a Dean at the University of Denver puts it: Diversity is an "imperative" and the university "community" must be "empowered" by its strategic plan "to build a foundation of diversity, equity and inclusive excellence towards becoming a national leader in culture, practices and structures that encourage inclusivity" (McIntosh, 2016). Given the description of diversity as an "imperative" and its close association with emotive terms such as "mission," "vision," and "community," we think it reasonable to treat diversity as a fantasy: a depiction of an imagined world shaped by deeply embedded desires and fears.

The diversity fantasy draws us in two opposing directions. On one side, it directs us toward the ideal of living in a society that includes people who are not like us, including those who are strangers to us. In this "civil" society, we live with people we do not know, at least not in the way we know those who share our beliefs and our ways of life. Since we do not know them in this way, we do not care about them, in the usual sense of the term, nor do they care about us. Yet we live with them and depend on them. We share our world with them, and we engage them in ways appropriate to sharing a world that is not solely "ours."

On the other side, the diversity fantasy represents a retreat from this understanding of civil society and even a protest against it. This aspect of the fantasy is most evident in the language of "community," invoked so frequently in discussions of diversity, and in the insistence that we *do* care or *must* care about those who differ from us, including those we do not know. If our relations with strangers were imbued with the caring normally reserved for those like us, there would be, in effect, no civil society. When the diversity fantasy operates in this second way, it reflects the desire to make society into a place that is not essentially different from the world we inhabited before we encountered strangers.

Although the "diverse community" includes people *un*like us and people we do not know, it also envisions itself as a "community" or group, formed by the bond characteristic of communities and groups: the bond of identification. The bond of identification is, as we have discussed above, one way of knowing others. Through it, we experience others as ourselves so that together we form one corporate entity. If we do not identify with those with whom we share the world, then our emotional attachment to them, if it exists at all, is highly attenuated.

As we have seen, much of the current strife within the university is rooted in a desire (frequently but not exclusively articulated by students) to establish "safe spaces." The "safety" of these spaces is thought to derive from the fact that, in them, strangers will not be encountered and, thus, those who occupy them can count on the bond of identification to shape relating. This desire to be saved from difference highlights a tension often exacerbated by diversity initiatives. This is the tension between (a) diversity as a requirement that we share our world with strangers we do not know, identify with, or care about, and (b) diversity as a demand that the university provide members with a "community" and a "space" that is made "safe" by the familiar bond of identification.

While this tension may be expressed in the language of diversity— with reference to the demographic and identity-based categories typically associated with diversity (such as race, ethnicity, gender, religion, sexual orientation, etc.)—it is not caused by the use of this language or by the initiatives associated with it, nor is it caused by the presence of the individuals and groups identified with these categories. Rather, the language, categories, and policies of diversity are best understood as expressions of a more fundamental tension between living in civil society and regressing into the familiar world of the group. This is not to say that the presence of an increasingly diverse student body is of no importance, but only that the impact of changes in the composition of the student body will only be well understood when placed in the larger context of the location of the university experience in the student's maturational process. Indeed, given the "place" of the university in that process (see the Introduction), tensions regarding entry into civil society are all but inevitable, as are the backward and forward movements associated with relating to and distancing ourselves from people exiting outside the bonds of family and group life.

As we have suggested throughout this book, ambivalence about living in a world of strangers is, at the same time, ambivalence about identity. Ambivalence about identity is ambivalence about the possibility of forming an identity expressive of the individual's original vitality and presence of being. It is also ambivalence about the standing of the individual's identity in a civil society, which is to say in a world where identity is not held in common. It is no easy matter to establish an identity that is positively invested *and* different from the identities of others. Yet, the less we are able to make a positive investment in our identity, the more acutely we will experience our ambivalence about the value of our selves, and the more powerful will be our impulse to move doubt about our value outside, holding those who differ from us responsible for it.

But if we displace and (re)discover the cause of our ambivalent investment in our identity outside—in the way others relate to us—we find the world of those who differ from us to be an unsafe place. If we respond to this predicament by seeking safe spaces to shield us from those who do not share our identity, then diversity initiatives that operate along these lines (ironically) sponsor sameness rather than difference, at least for those groups of students authorized by the institution to seek out like-minded communities.

At the same time, diversity initiatives driven by the diversity fantasy encourage students' identification with a bad self. This is the self that generates doubt about the value of identity, doubt from which the safe space of the group offers protection. Thus, when the university provides safe spaces as places of refuge from difference, it colludes not only with students' desires to retreat into communities of sameness, but also with students' ambivalence about the value of their identities. When this happens, the university's attempt to respond to the "imperative" of diversity leads it to obviate its task of preparing students to live in a world outside of family and community.

It is true that students' emotional survival depends, at least to some extent, on opportunities to retreat into spaces where the task of managing life with strangers can be suspended. This need is felt by all students, and, indeed, by all university members to varying degrees. It cannot be simply dismissed or treated differently for different groups of students without fostering conflict detrimental to the university's mission of teaching and learning. There is, however, an alternative to encouraging regression into identity groups as a way of providing students a retreat from the society of strangers. This alternative is to provide students opportunities for retreat into spaces made "safe" because it is possible there to escape the world of relating.

We cannot devote all our energies to relating to others, especially where our primary task is to engage in a process of learning that is, to a significant degree, all about turning inward. If we understand the "safety" of spaces to be correlated with the possibility of "turning inward" in them, then spaces limited to those who are like us are not really safe. They are not safe because, while in them, we suspend connection with what is unique about us so that we can participate in a group that shares an identity.

As we have noted, the movement in the direction of safe spaces, when understood as a retreat from difference into groups held together by identification, has gone hand in hand with a redefinition of learning, and even of thinking, in universities. By the terms of these redefinitions, learning and thinking have been understood less as internal processes, and more as processes that take place in groups. When this happens, the confusion of learning and thinking with group processes deprives students of vitally important educational experiences. The confusion of learning and thinking with group processes is a crucial part of the attack on the self underway in contemporary universities that we have sought to highlight in this book.

Leaving home

If "safety" is taken to mean being with others who are like us, then it means being kept safe not only from strangers, but also from contact with our selves. The impulse to keep the self at a safe distance begins early in life and can be considered a part of a fantasy that precedes the diversity fantasy and is, in a sense, its earliest and most primitive form. We will refer to this as the "school fantasy." The school fantasy can tell us something important about the diversity fantasy, especially why it draws us to a communal past that, while seeming idyllic, has a dark side.

By the phrase, "school fantasy," we refer to an interpretation of the experience of leaving home. In the world outside the home, the child encounters strangers—people not already known—and finds in them incarnations of the roles of parents and other significant figures who are already known. To be "already known" means to have already taken shape in the mind. For the child, figures who have already taken shape in the mind are fantasy figures who represent internalized relationships. These internalized fantasy relationships are experienced as "good" or "bad" depending on their roles in providing or withholding gratification. Of course, the child also knows himself on the basis of a fantasy of gratification in which the self is either deserving of gratification ("good") or an obstacle to it ("bad"). In other words, projection at this stage is projection of good and bad fantasy figures, or internal objects, and of the good and bad self.

The fantasies active in the school setting can be fantasies of the repair of those figures and of the world they jointly constitute. In these fantasies the bad figures are either made good or they are purged from the world. This work we do to repair or eliminate important figures in our earliest experiences of relating can be transferred via projection onto our way of relating to strangers. Transferring the family drama onto the stage of our life with strangers in the school setting is what we have in mind by the school fantasy.

The version of the school fantasy with which we are primarily concerned here drives an engagement with strangers that involves a struggle against their presence in our world or a flight from them into a world made safe by their absence. Where projection of bad fantasy figures onto the people encountered at school makes it a dangerous place, the result is an orientation toward the school dominated by fight or flight impulses. Preoccupation with making the school a safe place can encourage the playing out of a projective drama of the kind referred to above and can foster conflict when its purpose is to rid the school of conflict. Where fight or flight impulses dominate, the school setting will not be conducive to its primary task.

Central to a more positive experience of the school is the availability to the child of what Winnicott refers to as a benign environment in the inner world. A benign environment is made that way by the internalization of early relationships with parents who do a good enough job of adapting to the child's emotional needs. Once a nurturing or facilitating relationship has been internalized, the child is emotionally prepared to cope with a world in which the parent is not present, but where others—who are not the parent—are. This is because the role of the nurturing object can be played out internally, within the child's fantasy life, and, as a result, others are not depended on to play that role. Here, it is possible to contain good and bad fantasies internally, rather than to project them outside, because good feelings about the self are strong enough to withstand awareness of the bad.

When figures in the inner world are predominantly bad, however, and the self experienced there is predominantly bad, the internal environment is harsh, unforgiving, and anxiety-provoking. Coping with such an internal environment requires getting rid of bad internal objects and the bad self via projection. Characters encountered outside are then experienced as bad objects and the world outside is known as a dangerous place. This situation indicates the presence of a fantasy about the school as a place populated with threatening figures. School fantasies of this kind—which encourage projective dramas and "fight or flight" impulses—make learning, thinking, and relating in school difficult.

The problem of dominance of the inner world by bad objects arises either because the parent has failed to provide a sufficiently facilitating environment for the child, or because the parent has provided such an environment but has not sustained it long enough to allow it to be fully internalized. In either case, the lack or loss of the needed connection to the parent provokes fear and aggression in the child, and these emotions become dangerous objects in fantasy life, playing important roles in internal dramas. The more these dangerous objects dominate the inner world, the less that world affords the child a "safe" or benign environment into which he can retreat, and the less prepared the child will be (a) to undertake the kind of learning that calls for a retreat from relating and (b) to relate to others in ways that are not dominated by fear and aggression.

When the inner world of the child is not a "safe" place to be, it matters little how "safe" or "good" the school is to which she is sent. In other words, regardless of the "quality" of the school and its staff, the school will be experienced by the child as a place populated by bad objects. If the child finds herself in school before she is "ready" — "ready" in the sense of having adequately internalized a benign environment—the school will be experienced as a dangerous place and will place excessive demands on the child's limited emotional resources. The only way for the child to manage what will seem to be a threatening situation will be to mobilize primitive fantasies and defenses that impede self-contact and make the formation of healthy and productive relationships difficult.

Diversity and morality

In describing the school fantasy, we have highlighted the early experience of being thrown into a world of strangers when the internal resources for coping with that world are not adequate to the task. This experience generates dark fantasies and primitive defenses. The diversity fantasy can be considered the heir to these dark fantasies and defenses. In the diversity fantasy, what is asked of the student is that he mobilize defenses originally developed in response to early experiences and the dangerous emotions attached to them: specifically, that he use external figures to manage internal bad objects. In the diversity fantasy, the individual is encouraged to think and relate in precisely this way.

Under the sway of the diversity fantasy, the student is encouraged, if not forced, to put in place what Fairbairn refers to as the "moral defense" (1952), which manages internal bad objects by treating the self as a bad object. After all, the emotional experience associated with the diversity fantasy is that of finding oneself in a world of strangers, of feelings of confusion, isolation, fear, and aggression, and, then, of being told that any difficult emotions experienced in diverse settings represent moral failings resulting from the presence of a bad self.

Although treating the self as a bad object "saves" others in the world from badness, it also promotes an impulse to move the bad self outside. Among the ways this may be accomplished, one involves engaging in various kinds of "training," in which the individual is taught to become different from and better than she was before, in which she is imagined to be remade into something else, something not bad (for a fuller discussion of training, see also Bowker & Levine, 2016). The idea of diversity training thus reveals something essential about the relation of diversity to the moral defense and the fantasies and defenses linked to it.

Diversity rhetoric fits these fantasies, defenses, and strategies well when, by conscious intent or not, it assumes that students come to the university ill-prepared to share their world with strangers, and, therefore, that students will be intolerant of difference until taught or trained to think and behave otherwise. In this respect, as in others, the diversity fantasy presumes the identification of students with their bad selves. The university then offers students a way of managing their bad selves, first by accepting and affirming their identification with it, and, second, by asking them to retrain themselves and to rectify their badness in part by remaining ever-vigilant about their own and others' moral failings.

This last message is clearly conveyed in the popular conviction that being able to live in a diverse world is essentially a matter of confronting students with the realities of diversity as a moral lesson, which is the point of many diversity initiatives. Understood as moral lessons, university rhetoric about diversity tends to adopt an aggressively moral tone, one that seems to express a desire within the university to make itself a moral beacon. Operating in this emotional context, diversity initiatives, whatever else they may represent, psychologically repeat the early experience of being sent into the world of school and school-like experiences. This experience entails fear, loss, and anger, and results in the development of defenses that impair our capacity to relate to self and others in ways that are respectful of difference. Of the many ironies in this dilemma, one that stands out is that this experience is imposed on students for *their own good*. In other words, the diversity fantasy implies that moral improvement results from being sent, ill-prepared, into a world of strangers and from developing defenses against the destructive impulses provoked by that experience.

The alternative to engaging the diversity fantasy would be to emphasize, within the university, the provision of support for the self, and the provision of literal and figurative "spaces" that are safe, because, in them, it is safe to be in contact with the self. This alternative cannot be made consistent, however, with the university's moral orientation to diversity nor with the "moral defense" it sponsors in students. So long as diversity initiatives are organized around an unconscious fantasy of the kind to which Fairbairn draws our attention, they cannot establish genuinely safe spaces. Instead, they are likely to diminish, rather than enhance, students' capacities to make contact with the self.

It is not always easy to discern when a university experience will help prepare students for life in a world where relating is governed by factors other than group identification, or when, instead, it will solidify group identity by making group dynamics stand in for learning, thinking, and living. Nevertheless, it may be said that celebrating different, local, or particular cultures and identity-based group-affiliations is, at best, a problematic solution to the difficulties facing universities. Such celebrations tend to entrench group connections, and may stand in the way of individuals' efforts to free themselves from the world of groups and to explore a world of others conceived as individuals living, to some degree, outside of groups. While such celebrations generally appear benign, they do not help (and may well hinder) individuals in their efforts to secure a meaningful degree of independence from groups that would claim to define their identities and to determine what is real and valuable in their lives.

To assist individuals in securing freedom and independence, universities would have to devote energy not to supporting diversity, but to supporting and strengthening what resilience the student brings with him when he enrolls. The more resilient the student, in the sense of the word used here, the greater the student's aptitude for learning, especially the kind of learning that engages his creative capacities. Under pressure from students (and other university members) to provide safe spaces for archaic connections and group-oriented experiences of self and other, universities have too often accepted measures that undermine students' aspirations to establish autonomy in living, which requires that they make the self, rather than the group, the center of their doing and relating.

Ambivalence and hope

To live and thrive in a world outside family and community, we must give up the hope that we can remake our world, in this case the university, into a community of people "like us." This means we must give up the hope that retreating into our group identities will be all we need to make our way in the world. There is ample evidence, in their responses to student demands, that university faculty and administrators are engaged with this hope, which is the hope that civil society can be eliminated or, at least, that it can be transformed into something akin to a community or group. The fantasy of eliminating civil society or transforming it into a community or group also transforms the primary goal of the university so that its task is no longer one of enabling students to live in a world of those who differ from them, but, rather, of supporting them in their belief that they can transform the world by eliminating difference from it.

To the degree that what we value about ourselves is our attachment to an identity-based group, we will experience the world outside family, group, or community as a dangerous place to be. The diversity fantasy contains both the expectation that we will move beyond our group of common identity *and* the hope that we need not enter into a way of being and relating for which no guidance is provided by our group. These hopes apply as well to those groups and organizations (such as the "diverse community" of the university) that treat diversity itself as an object that binds members via identification and shared belief.

Although projective defenses against ambivalence about the self permit us to mitigate tension and anxiety, they also reflect a desire to "hold onto" the eliminated feelings and desires, even when "holding onto" them means replaying them in enactments or identifications with others. In this book, we have described ambivalence about identity, self-determination, home, civil society, diversity, and more. The presence of these powerful ambivalences suggests that it would be naive to assume that university conflict is something that those in the university simply or unequivocally wish to resolve.

On one level, an individual student or group may demand change to resolve a contentious issue or to rectify an injustice. But on another level, a student or group may make a demand in a way that suggests that the (equally important) opposing intent behind it is to hold onto feelings of dissatisfaction, injustice, anger, or grief. Making demands that are impossible to satisfy, demands that are internally contradictory, or demands that contain a substantial amount of aggression (and, so, are likely to provoke aggressive responses in those who receive them) may all be expressions of ambivalence.

On this matter, we might recall how, in fantasies of victimization operative in university conflict, danger is paradoxically *required* in order to feel secure in the belief that one is endangered, a belief that binds together groups that conceive of themselves as endangered, victimized, excluded, or oppressed. In this case, even though the group experiences victimization as a threat to its existence, the same victimization must be realized (and must even be perpetuated) in the university in order to keep the group alive. That is, the group requires danger in order to keep the group's ambivalent hope alive: the hope that it will both conquer its victimizers and yet remain a group that can know its members and others via shared fantasies of victimization.

Of course, observers may be tempted to judge these ambivalent expressions, and the individuals and groups that voice them, to be foolish, childish, or mad. But to do so would be to collude with the dramas involved, rather than to understand them. To understand the nature of these ambivalent wishes, universities must strive to see their connections to more complex conflicts surrounding identity that make both the resolution of identity-related strife and the failure to resolve identity-related strife untenable outcomes. Faced with these contradictions, we find ourselves in a situation in which university members devote themselves to the vigilant monitoring and judgment of others' (and their own) thoughts and expressions concerning identity. This stance reflects a fear of discovering, and a hope of discovering, damning flaws within the self. Our alignment with forces of surveillance, control, and punishment, then, both relies on and reinforces our conviction that we are flawed and in need of supervision, correction, and the support of identity-defining groups lest what is bad within us rise up to be seen by ourselves and others.

While we cannot hope that the university will overcome all regressive forces, we can encourage the university to take measures that limit regression in the formulation and implementation of policy. These measures would involve not the vigilant monitoring, exposing, and censuring of university members, but, rather, sustained efforts to understand the fantasies embedded in the goals of university policies and university protests. Awareness and understanding of fantasies that undermine students' capacities to live in a world of difference can strengthen the university's own resilience, which is to say, its capacity to resist collusion with regressive tendencies. Greater awareness and understanding will not eliminate the contradictions embedded in policy or protest, nor will they eradicate conflict on university campuses, but they may increase the likelihood that activities undertaken by university members will facilitate thinking, learning, and genuine student development.

REFERENCES

American Association of University Professors (AAUP). (2014). On trigger warnings. www.aaup.org/report/trigger-warnings (last accessed January 11, 2017).

Arnett, J. (2000). Emerging adulthood: A theory of development from the late teens through the twenties. *American Psychologist, 55*(5): 469–480.

Barack, L., Mintz, S., & Emba, C. (2014). Higher education in the 21st century: Meeting real-world demands. *The Economist.* www.economistinsights. com/sites/default/files/EIU_AcademicPartns_WEBr1.pdf (last accessed January 11, 2017).

Beauvoir, S. (1949). *Le deuxième sexe.* Paris: Gallimard.

Benjamin, W. (2003). On the concept of history. In: H. Eiland & M. Jennings (Eds.), *Benjamin: Selected Writings, Vol. IV: 1938–1940* (pp. 389–400) (E. Jephcott et al. Trans.). Cambridge, MA and London: Belknap.

Blackmore, P., & Kandiko, C. (Eds.) (2012). *Strategic Curriculum Change in Universities: Global Trends.* New York: Routledge.

Bloom, A. (1987). *The Closing of the American Mind.* New York: Simon & Schuster.

Bollas, C. (1989). *Forces of Destiny: Psychoanalysis and the Human Idiom.* London: Free Association.

Bowker, M. (2012). Defending the ivory tower: Toward critical community-engagement. *Thought and Action: The NEA Higher Education Journal, 28*(1): 106–117.

Bowker, M. (2014). *Rethinking the Politics of Absurdity: Albert Camus, Postmodernity, and the Survival of Innocence.* New York and London: Routledge.

Bowker, M. (2016). *Ideologies of Experience: Trauma, Failure, Deprivation, and the Abandonment of the Self.* New York and London: Routledge.

Bowker, M. (2017). Review: *America at War with Itself,* by Henry A. Giroux. *Logos: A Journal of Modern Society and Culture, 16*(1). http://logosjournal. com/.

Bowker, M., & Buzby, A. (Eds.) (2017). *D.W. Winnicott and Political Theory: Recentering the Subject.* New York: Palgrave Macmillan.

Bowker, M., & Fazioli, K. (2016). Rethinking critical thinking: A relational and practical approach. *Pedagogy and the Human Sciences, 6*(1): 1–26.

Bowker, M., & Levine, D. (2016). Beyond the battlefield: 'Moral injury' and moral defense in the psychic life of the soldier, the military, and the nation. *Organisational and Social Dynamics, 16*(2): 85–109.

Boyington, B. (2014). Make a large college feel like home. *US News and World Report.* www.usnews.com/education/best-colleges/articles/2014/ 08/13/make-a-large-college-feel-like-home (last accessed January 11, 2017).

Bracher, M. (2006). *Radical Pedagogy Identity, Generativity, and Social Transformation.* New York: Palgrave.

Brown, E. (2015). Classical mythology too triggering for Columbia students. *Reason.* http://reason.com/blog/2015/05/12/trigger-warning-mythology (last accessed January 11, 2017).

Camus, A. (1956). *The Rebel: An Essay on Man in Revolt.* A. Bower (Trans.). New York: Vintage.

Caruth, C. (1995). Introduction. In: C. Caruth (Ed.), *Trauma: Explorations in Memory* (pp. 1–12). Baltimore, MD: Johns Hopkins University Press.

Caruth, C. (1996). *Unclaimed Experience: Trauma, Narrative, and History.* Baltimore, MD: Johns Hopkins University Press.

Chan, M. (2015). University at Buffalo student hangs 'White Only' signs on campus, sparks outrage. *New York Daily News.* September 18. www. nydailynews.com/news/national/university-buffalo-student-hangs-white-signs-article-1.2366089 (last accessed January 11, 2017).

Clark-Billings, L. (2015). Germaine Greer in transgender rant: 'Just because you lop off your penis ... it doesn't make you a woman.' *The Telegraph.* www.telegraph.co.uk/news/health/news/11955891/Germaine-Greer-in-transgender-rant-Just-because-you-lop-off-your-penis...it-doesnt-make-you-a-woman.html (last accessed January 11, 2017).

Columbia University Athletics. (2016). Columbia Athletics statement on Wrestling Program. www.gocolumbialions.com/ViewArticle.dbml?DB_OEM_ID=9600&ATCLID=211305803 *(last accessed January 2, 2017)*.

Cooney, S. (2016). Princeton suspends its Swimming and Diving Team for misogynistic messages. *Motto.* http://motto.time.com/4604724/princeton-swimming-misogynistic-messages/ (last accessed January 11, 2017).

Courtney, N. (2009). *Academic Library Outreach: Beyond the Campus Walls.* Westport, CT: Libraries Unlimited.

Courtois, C., Sonis, J., Brown, L., Cook, J., Fairbank, J., Friedman, M., Gone, J., Jones, R., La Greca, A., Mellman, T., Roberts, J., & Schulz, P. (2016). Clinical practice guideline for the treatment of posttraumatic stress disorder (PTSD) in Adults. (Draft). Guideline Development Panel for PTSD Treatment of the American Psychological Association. http://apacustomout.apa.org/commentPracGuidelines/Practice/Full%20PTSD%20text%20clean%2010-4-16%20 revised.pdf (last accessed January 11, 2017).

Curtis, D. (2001). Project-based learning: Real-world issues motivate students. *Edutopia: What Works in Education. George Lucas Educational Foundation.* www.edutopia.org/project-based-learning-student-motivation (last accessed January 11, 2017).

Dartmouth College. (2015). Collaborative learning/learning with peers. Institute for Writing and Rhetoric. https://writing-speech.dartmouth.edu/teaching/first-year-writing-pedagogies-methods-design/collaborative-learninglearning-peers (last accessed December 30, 2016).

Deci, E., & Ryan, R. (1985). *Intrinsic Motivation and Self-Determination in Human Behavior.* New York: Plenum.

Delgado-Guerrero, M., Cherniack, M., & Gloria, A. (2014). Family away from home: Factors influencing undergraduate women of color's decision to join a cultural-specific sorority. *Journal of Diversity in Higher Education, 7*: 45–57.

Diamond, M. A. (1991). Stresses of group membership: Balancing the need for independence and belonging. In: M. Kets de Vries & Associates (Eds.), *Organizations on the Couch: Clinical Perspectives on Organizational Behavior and Change* (pp. 191–214). San Francisco: Jossey-Bass.

Diamond, M. A. (2017). *Discovering Organizational Identity: Dynamics of Relational Attachment.* Columbia and London: University of Missouri Press.

Ditum, S. (2014). 'No platform' was once reserved for violent fascists. Now it's being used to silence debate. *New Statesman.* March 18. www.newstatesman.com/sarah-ditum/2014/03/when-did-no-platform-become-about-attacking-individuals-deemed-disagreeable (last accessed January 11, 2017).

Drezner, D. (2015). A clash between administrators and students at Yale went viral. Why that is unfortunate for all concerned: The trouble with 21st century campus politics. *The Washington Post*. November 9. www.washingtonpost.com/posteverything/wp/2015/11/09/a-clash-between-administrators-and-students-at-yale-went-viral-why-that-is-unfortunate-for-all-concerned/?utm_term=.88664f5e0e72 (last accessed January 11, 2017).

Duckworth, A., Peterson, C., Matthews, M., & Kelly, D. (2007). Grit: Perseverance and passion for long-term goals. *Journal of Personality and Social Psychology, 92*(6): 1087–1101.

Economist, The (2012). Higher education not what it used to be: American universities represent declining value for money to their students. www.economist.com/news/united-states/21567373-american-universities-represent-declining-value-money-their-students-not-what-it (last accessed January 11, 2017).

Fairbairn, W. R. D. (1952). The repression and the return of bad objects. In: *Psychoanalytic Studies of the Personality* (pp. 59–81). New York and London: Tavistock and Routledge.

Fassin, D., & Rechtman, R. (2009). *The Empire of Trauma: An Inquiry into the Condition of Victimhood*. Princeton, NJ: Princeton University Press.

Felman, S. (1995). Education and crisis, or the vicissitudes of teaching. In: C. Caruth (Ed.), *Trauma: Explorations in Memory* (pp. 13–60). Baltimore, MD: Johns Hopkins University Press.

Felman, S., & Laub, D. (1992). *Testimony: Crises of Witnessing in Literature, Psychoanalysis, and History*. New York: Taylor & Francis.

Foran, C. (2015). When one student's art is another's aggression: A black student posted 'White Only' signs on water fountains to highlight systemic racism—and provoked an uproar. *The Atlantic Online*. December 1. www.theatlantic.com/politics/archive/2015/12/art-on-campus/418116/? (last accessed December 23, 2016).

Friedersdorf, C. (2015). The new intolerance of student activism. *The Atlantic*. www.theatlantic.com/politics/archive/2015/11/the-new-intolerance-of-student-activism-at-yale/414810/ (last accessed January 11, 2017).

Friedersdorf, C. (2016). Left outside the social-justice movement's small tent. *The Atlantic*. www.theatlantic.com/politics/archive/2016/04/outside-the-socialjustice-movements-small-tent/479049/ (last accessed April 25, 2016).

Garshfield, J. (2015). UCSB's free speech problem. *Daily Nexus*. http://dailynexus.com/2015–10–01/ucsbs-free-speech-problem/ (last accessed January 11, 2017).

Godsey, M. (2015). When schools overlook introverts. *The Atlantic*. www.theatlantic.com/education/archive/2015/09/introverts-at-school-overlook/407467/ (last accessed December 30, 2016).

Goldberg, J. (2015). Campus commotions show we're raising fragile kids. *The National Review.* www.nationalreview.com/article/426853/campus-commotions-show-were-raising-fragile-kids-jonah-goldberg (last accessed January 11, 2017).

Gornitzka, A. (1999). Governmental policies and organisational change in higher education. *Higher Education, 38*(1): 5–31.

Gray, P. (2015). Declining student resilience: A serious problem for colleges. *Psychology Today.* www.psychologytoday.com/blog/freedom-learn/201509/declining-student-resilience-serious-problem-colleges (last accessed January 11, 2017).

Green, A. (2016). The cost of balancing academia and racism. *The Atlantic.* www.theatlantic.com/education/archive/2016/01/balancing-academia-racism/424887/?google_editors_picks=true (last accessed January 21, 2016).

Greenberg, J. (1986). The problem of analytic neutrality. *Contemporary Psychoanalysis, 22*: 76–86.

Harter, S. (1999). Symbolic interactionism revisited: Potential liabilities for the self constructed in the crucible of interpersonal relationships. *Merrill-Palmer Quarterly, 45*: 677–703.

Hayden, T. (2014a). UCSB Professor sentenced to probation, community service in theft, battery case. August 18. *Santa Barbara Independent.* www.independent.com/news/2014/aug/18/ucsb-professor-sentenced-probation-community-servi/ (last accessed January 11, 2017).

Hayden, T. (2014b). UCSB Police Department releases professor-protestor incident report. March 18. *Santa Barbara Independent.* www.independent.com/news/2014/mar/18/ucsb-police-department-releases-professor-protesto/ (last accessed January 11, 2017).

Hayward, J. (2015). Campus special snowflakes melt upon contact with Greek mythology. www.breitbart.com/big-government/2015/05/12/campus-special-snowflakes-melt-upon-contact-with-greek-mythology/ (last accessed January 11, 2017).

Hettich P. (2010). College-to-workplace transitions: Becoming a freshman again. In: T. Miller (Ed.), *Handbook of Stressful Transitions Across the Lifespan* (pp. 87–109). New York: Springer.

Jarvie, J. (2014). Trigger happy. *The New Republic.* https://newrepublic.com/article/116842/trigger-warnings-have-spread-blogs-college-classes-thats-bad (last accessed January 11, 2017).

Johnson, K., Lynch, T., Monroe, E., & Wang, T. (2015). Our identities matter in Core classrooms. http://columbiaspectator.com/opinion/2015/04/30/our-identities-matter-core-classrooms (last accessed January 11, 2017).

Kafele, B. (2013). *Closing the Attitude Gap: How to Fire up Your Students to Strive for Success.* Alexandria, VA: ACSD.

Kirchik, J. (2016). New videos show how Yale betrayed itself by favoring cry-bullies. *Tablet.* www.tabletmag.com/jewish-news-and-politics/213212/yale-favoring-cry-bullies (last accessed January 11, 2017).

Kohut, H. (1977). *The Restoration of the Self.* Chicago, IL: University of Chicago Press.

Kolb, A., & Kolb, D. (2009). Experiential learning theory: A dynamic, holistic approach to management learning, education and development. In: S. Armstrong & C. Fukami (Eds.), *The Sage Handbook of Management Learning, Education and Development* (pp. 42–68). London: Sage.

Laing, R. D. (1969). *The Divided Self: An Existential Study in Sanity and Madness.* London: Penguin.

Laplanche, J., & Pontalis, J.-B. (1973). *The Language of Psychoanalysis.* D. Nicholson-Smith (Trans.). New York: Norton.

Lee, P. (2011). The curious life of *in loco parentis* in American universities. *Higher Education in Review, 8:* 65–90.

Levine, D. (2003.) *The Living Dead and the End of Hope: An Essay on the Pursuit of Unhappiness.* Denver, CO: Broken Tree Press.

Levine, D. (2010). *Object Relations, Work, and the Self.* East Sussex: Routledge.

Levine, D. (2013). *The Capacity for Ethical Conduct: On Psychic Existence and the Way We Relate to Others.* Abingdon, Oxon: Routledge.

Levine, D. (2017). *Psychoanalysis, Society, and the Inner World: Embedded Meaning in Politics and Social Conflict.* Abingdon, Oxon: Routledge.

Lovell, E. (2014). The importance of black faculty. *The Chronicle.* February 28. www.dukechronicle.com/article/2014/02/importance-black-faculty (last accessed January 13, 2017).

Lukianoff, G., & Haidt, J. (2015). The coddling of the American mind. *The Atlantic.* www.theatlantic.com/magazine/archive/2015/09/the-coddling-of-the-american-mind/399356/ (last accessed January 11, 2017).

MacIntosh, D. (2016). University of Denver webpage. https://dughost.imodules.com/controls/email_marketing/admin/email_marketing_email_viewer.aspx?sid=1150&eiid=13793&seiid=7445&usearchive=1&puid=7c10525a-fb4e-4b65-b1b9-a2e35b723df5 (last accessed December 30, 2016).

Marcia, J. (1967). Ego identity status: relationship to change in self-esteem, 'general maladjustment,' and authoritarianism. *Journal of Personality, 35*(1): 118–133.

Martin, J., & Grubic, A. (2016). Columbia University halts wrestling program amid investigation into lewd texts. November 15. *CNN.* http://edition.cnn.com/2016/11/15/sport/columbia-wrestling-season-on-hold-amid-investigation/ (last accessed January 11, 2017).

McGettigan, A. (2013). *The Great University Gamble: Money, Markets and the Future of Higher Education.* London: Pluto.

McLoughlin, E. (2015). Report: University of Oklahoma student apologizes for racist chant. *CNN*. March 10. www.cnn.com/2015/03/10/us/oklahoma-racist-chant/ (last accessed January 11, 2017).

McNally, R. (2016). If you need a trigger warning, you need PTSD treatment. *The New York Times*. September 13. www.nytimes.com/roomfordebate/2016/09/13/do-trigger-warnings-work/if-you-need-a-trigger-warning-you-need-ptsd-treatment (last accessed January 11, 2017).

Menzies, I. (1960). A case study in the functioning of social systems as a defense against anxiety. *Human Relations, 13*: 95–121.

Moore, V. (2015). Beyond the campus walls and into the community. http://news.furman.edu/2015/03/20/beyond-the-campus-walls-and-into-the-community/ (last accessed December 30, 2016).

National Coalition Against Censorship. (2015). NCAC report: What's all this about trigger warnings? http://ncac.org/wp-content/uploads/2015/11/NCAC-TriggerWarningReport.pdf (last accessed January 11, 2017).

Nisbet, R. (1971). *The Degradation of the Academic Dogma: The University in America (1945 – 1970)*. London and New York: Basic.

O'Neill, B. (2015). The 'Yale snowflakes': Who made these monsters? www.spiked-online.com/newsite/article/the-yale-snowflakes-who-made-these-monsters/17613#.WHmRsVMrIdU (last accessed January 11, 2017).

Pao, P.-N. (1983). Therapeutic empathy and the treatment of schizophrenics. *Psychoanalytic Inquiry, 3*: 145–67.

Racker, H. (1968). *Transference and Countertransference*. London: Karnac.

Reagan, L. (2013). Our home away from home: Putting a stop to college campus violence. *Artifacts* 8. https://artifactsjournal.missouri.edu/2013/05/our-home-away-from-home-putting-a-stop-to-college-campus-violence/ *(last accessed January 11, 2017)*.

Sagaria, M. (2007). *Women, Universities, and Change: Gender Equality in the European Union and the United States*. New York: Palgrave Macmillan.

Schafer, R. (1983). *The Analytic Attitude*. New York: Basic.

Schrecker, E. (2010). *The Lost Soul of Higher Education: Corporatization, the Assault on Academic Freedom, and the End of the American University*. New York: New Press.

Shaffer, L., & Zalewski, J. (2011). It's what I have always wanted to do: Advising the foreclosure student. *The NACADA Journal, 31*(2): 62–77.

Shay, J. (1995). *Achilles in Vietnam: Combat Trauma and the Undoing of Character*. New York: Simon and Schuster.

Soave, R. (2015). *In loco parentis* returns: Yale and Mizzou students want to be treated like kids again. *Reason.com*. https://reason.com/blog/2015/11/09/yale-missouri-students-speech-college (last accessed January 11, 2017).

Southall, A., & Bohan, C. (2014). Helping ESOL students find their voice in social studies. *Georgia Social Studies Journal, 4*(1): 1–9.

Staley, D., & Trinkle, D. (2011). The changing landscape of higher education. *Educause Review, 46*(1): 16–32.

Stanley-Becker, I. (2015). Hundreds march at Yale in solidarity with minority students. *The Washington Post*. November 9. www.washingtonpost. com/news/grade-point/wp/2015/11/09/hundreds-march-at-yale-in-solidarity-with-minority-students/?utm_term=.64640eeec99b (last accessed January 11, 2017).

Strayhorn, T., Terrell, M., Redmond, J., & Walton, C. (2010). A home away from home: Black cultural centers as supportive environments for African American collegians at white institutions. In: M. C. Terrell, & T. L. Strayhorn (Eds.), *The Evolving Challenges of Black College Students: New Insights for Practice, and Research* (pp. 122–137). Sterling, VA: Stylus.

Svetlik, D. (2007). When the academic world and the real world meet. *Thought and Action: The NEA Higher Education Journal, 23*(1): 47–55.

Svrluga, S. (2015). OU: Frat members learned racist chant at national SAE leadership event. *The Washington Post*. March 27. www.washington-post.com/news/grade-point/wp/2015/03/27/ou-investigation-sae-members-learned-racist-chant-at-national-leadership-event/? utm_term=.05e4ba37ca37 (last accessed January 11, 2017).

Thompson, C., & Walsh, G. (2015). Missouri would likely stand alone with 10 percent black faculty; Other flagships much lower. November 17. www.usnews.com/news/us/articles/2015/11/17/missouri-would-likely-be-alone-with-10-percent-black-faculty (last accessed January 11, 2017).

Tobacyk, J. (1981). Personality differentiation, effectiveness of personality integration, and mood in female college students. *Journal of Personality and Social Psychology, 41*: 348–356.

Turley, J. (2014). Professor Miller-Young sentenced to probation and anger management classes for attack on pro-life advocates. https:// jonathanturley.org/2014/08/18/professor-miller-young-sentenced-to-probation-and-anger-management-classes-for-attack-on-pro-life-advocates/ (last accessed January 11, 2017).

Twenge, J. (2006). *Generation Me: Why Today's Young Americans are More Confident, Assertive, Entitled – and More Miserable than Ever Before*. New York: Free Press.

Twenge, J., & Campbell, W. (2009). *The Narcissism Epidemic: Living in the Age of Entitlement*. New York: Simon and Schuster.

UCSB Police Department. (2014). University of California, Santa Barbara Police Department Crime Report (Redacted). March 4. http://media.

independent.com/news/documents/2014/03/18/UCSB-Police-Report.pdf (last accessed January 11, 2017).

Vivanco, L., & Rhodes, D. (2016). U. of C. tells incoming freshmen it does not support 'trigger warnings' or 'safe spaces.' *The Chicago Tribune*. August 25. www.chicagotribune.com/news/local/breaking/ct-university-of-chicago-safe-spaces-letter-met-20160825-story.html (last accessed January 11, 2017).

Volokh, E. (2014). UC Santa Barbara professor steals young anti-abortion protester's sign, apparently assaults protesters, says she 'set a good example for her students'. March 20. *The Washington Post*. www.washingtonpost.com/news/volokh-conspiracy/wp/2014/03/20/uc-santa-barbara-professor-steals-young-anti-abortion-protesters-sign-apparently-assaults-protesters-says-she-set-a-good-example-for-her-students/?utm_term=.f1637c66fcbf (last accessed January 11, 2017).

Whetten, D. (2006). Albert and Whetten revisited: Strengthening the concept of organizational identity. *Journal of Management Inquiry, 15*(3): 219–234.

Williamson, K. (2015). Yale's idiot children. *The National Review*. www.nationalreview.com/article/426813/yales-idiot-children-kevin-d-williamson (last accessed January 11, 2017).

Winnicott, D. W. (1965). Ego distortions in terms of true and false self. In: *The Maturational Process and the Facilitating Environment*. New York: International Universities Press.

Winnicott, D. W. (1971). *Playing and Reality*. London: Routledge.

Winnicott, D. W. (1986). *Home is Where We Start From: Essays by a Psychoanalyst*. C. Winnicott, R. Shepard, & M. Davis (Eds.). New York: W.W. Norton.

Winnicott, D. W. (1989). *Psychoanalytic Explorations*. C. Winnicott, R. Shepard, & M. Davis (Eds.). Cambridge, MA: Harvard University Press.

Winnicott, D. W. (1990). *Deprivation and Delinquency*. C. Winnicott, R. Shepherd, & M. Davis (Eds.). London and New York: Routledge.

Worland, J. (2015). University of Oklahoma President condemns 'disgraceful' fraternity after racist video. March 9. http://time.com/3737345/ou-racist-video/ (last accessed January 11, 2017).

INDEX